"This book may be the most impor
its youth workers, for when utiliz
release of many gifts, both from ac
whom they minister."

"I have found Stephen Jones's book *Faith Shaping* to be a valuable resource both in youth ministry and Christian education classes in seminary and workshops with youth leaders of local churches. This revision and update only enhances and insures its continued usage."
—*Paul Nichols, Executive Director*
Board of National Ministries
American Baptist Churches in the U.S.A.

"*Faith Shaping* is a thought-provoking book that should be read by all those who are involved in the process of nurturing youth in their faith development. . . . I found this book to be . . . practical in terms of defining the steps required in the passing on of the faith from one generation to the next."
—*The Youth Leader Magazine*

"*Faith Shaping* offers a unique combination of conceptualization and practical strategies which transcends a particular cultural milieu. The book will be a helpful resource for effective youth ministry in multi-cultural settings."
—*Dr. Víctor M. Vázquez, Pastor*
Juncos, Puerto Rico

"Based on his own experiences in youth ministry, (Jones) presents a sequence and set of tasks descriptive of the journey of young people in coming to faith. His premise is that adults play a vital role in the shaping of faith in young people, and his book is designed to offer both theoretical understanding of this faith shaping and prac- tical suggestions as to what can be done to assist and not hinder youth in their journeys of faith. I highly recommend this book to anyone concerned about youth in the church today. It is one that I will use with my own students in their preparation for ministry with youth."
—*Karen Tye*
Associate Professor of Christian Education
Berkeley, California

FAITH
shaping

Stephen D. Jones

FAITH
shaping

youth
and the
experience
of
faith

revised

edition

Judson Press®
Valley Forge

Unless otherwise indicated, Bible quotations in this volume are from the Revised Standard Version of the Bible, copyrighted 1946, 1952 (c), 1971, 1973 by the Division of Christian Education of the National Council of the Churches of Christ in the U.S.A., and used by permission.

Other versions of the Bible quoted in this book are:

Good News Bible, the Bible in Today's English Version. Copyright (c) American Bible Society, 1976. Used by permission.

The New English Bible, Copyright (c) The Delegates of the Oxford University Press and The Syndics of the Cambridge University Press, 1961, 1970.

The Holy Bible, King James Version.

Library of Congress Cataloging-in-Publication Data
Jones, Stephen D.
    Faith shaping.

    1. Youth—Religious life.   2.Church work with youth.   I. Title.
BV4531.2.J64   1987   268'.433   87-3620
ISBN 0-8170-1118-8

Contents

FAITH
shaping

Preface

I first wrote *Faith Shaping* nine years ago. At twenty-eight years of age, I was involved as a young adult with many of the issues of my own adolescence still unraveling before my eyes! I was just to the point where, for the first time, I could face my childhood faith and accept it for what it was.

I hope the passion of my first attempt to describe the adolescent faith experience is still in this revised edition. But my ideas about faith and nurture have changed and deepened in the ensuing years, and those changes are reflected primarily in the first two new chapters. This has necessitated many other changes and other new chapters throughout the remainder of the book.

In many ways *Faith Shaping . . . Youth and the Experience of Faith* is a new book when compared to the original, *Faith Shaping . . . Nurturing the Faith Journey of Youth.*

I give thanks to God that the last nine years have afforded me the continued opportunity to observe and interact with youth. I will never fully understand them, nor do I necessarily even seek to, but I believe that I more deeply appreciate the important work of adolescence as the shaping of faith. As with the first edition, my focus is upon the years of adolescence—the transitional years. However, the childhood years as the foundation and the young adults years as the outgrowth are also explored.

I give thanks for the many groups to which I have spoken since *Faith Shaping* was first published. Those interactions not only in the United States but particularly in Canada and the Philippines have added invaluable insight and needed correction into the faith-shaping process.

I am a pastor as well as an educator, and both perspectives will be evident as you read these pages. I do not apologize that I write from involvement with youth and not from scientific analysis or abstract research, though both surely have their place. I am proud to have been called to the practice of ministry with youth, and that is my perspective.

For that reason, I give thanks to youth and adults in three churches that I have been privileged to pastor, for it was in these congregational contexts that I have served as one who nurtures and evangelizes with youth: the First Baptist Church of Boulder, Colorado; the First Baptist Church of Dayton, Ohio; and the Central Baptist Church of Wayne, Pennsylvania.

This book is dedicated to my wife, Jan, my lifelong partner in faith shaping!

Stephen D. Jones
Wayne, Pennsylvania

Faith and Ambiguity

Why did you have an accident, Daddy?" five-year-old Brian asked in his childlike innocence. "Wasn't it the truck's fault?" I had been driving through Tennessee on a family vacation and had failed to stop our car in time before crashing into the back of a slow-moving truck. For months following the accident and during an extended recuperation period for our family, Brian couldn't understand how I could have caused such an accident. "Brian, I made a mistake when I was driving," I would answer. But no matter what I would say or how often I would explain it, it was beyond Brian's comprehension. He remembered the accident, actually in a rather matter-of-fact way. But what he found unacceptable was that his daddy could make such a mistake. It was a faith issue for Brian. If a parent could make a mistake like that, then parents are not fully dependable nor can they be fully trusted.

The faith of a child is different from the faith of an adolescent or an adult. There are attributes of childlike faith that are worth emulating (Matthew 18:3)—the sense of wonder and discovery as well as the natural ability to think and explore with the imagination. But there is also a simplicity of faith in the childhood years that becomes simplistic when "force-fit" into the teen or young adult or middle adult years.

Where does adolescent faith begin? What causes the transformation from a childlike faith to a faith appropriate to the adolescent years?

For me it started with the opening of a door. For all the sons and daughters of Eve it starts at whatever moment it is at which the . . . timeless innocence of childhood ends, which may be either a dramatic moment, as it was for me, or a moment or series of moments so subtle and undramatic that we scarcely recognize them. But one way or another the journey through time starts for us all, . . . a journey *in search*. [1]

[1]Frederick Buechner, *The Sacred Journey* (New York: Harper & Row, Publishers Inc., 1982), p. 58.

A child's faith is most often characterized by a trust that rarely probes the assumptions upon which it rests. Even children's questions reflect an innocent trust in that which they have been taught to value. The faith of a teenager is a "journey in search." It is a journey that questions those childlike assumptions. Often this begins with the question in the mind of an eleven-year-old, or possibly a fourteen-year-old, which they haven't the nerve even to verbalize: "Why is this so?" or "Who says so?" or "Why doesn't this make more sense?" or "Who can be trusted?"

Ambiguity is at the heart of the adult experience. Adults have learned that life can be paradoxical—we are gifted with the ability to cope, yet often we encounter experiences with which we cannot cope; we are gifted with the ability to create an enjoyable life, yet often we face despair and disappointment; we have been gifted, yet often we feel rejection, or we reject ourselves.

> We search for a self to be. We search for other selves to love. We search for work to do. And since even when to one degree or another we find these things, we find also that there is still something crucial missing we have not found, we search for that unfound thing too, even though we do not know its name or where it is to be found or even if it is to be found at all."[2]

Adults have grown suspicious of "easy answers" because they have experienced the life span of easy answers! Adults know that life can be unfair. Adults know that situations and other persons are not always, nor even often, within their control. Adults know that failure cannot always be avoided. *Adults "know" these things whether they admit them or not.* For most of us, the childhood years eventually reveal this reality, *but it is not normally until adolescence that the full force of life's ambiguities is felt.*

Adult faith can be a diversion from the ambiguity. It is a fact true for all of us: we want to avoid the ambiguity implicit in the human situation. Sometimes we make faith claims that pretend the ambiguity doesn't exist. We might make such a statement as "God meets all my needs," even though such a belief reduces God to little more than a personal "errand girl." There could be little debate among Christians that God *could* meet all my needs at the moment I identify them, but the truth is that God doesn't do that. God doesn't respond on my time line, nor is God's will for my life based upon my perceptions or my will. It has often come as a shock to me, but the truth is that God's purpose in the universe is not to conform to my expectations. And therein lies the ambiguity. *Christian/biblical faith is an address to life's inherent ambiguities, not a diversion from them.*

[2]*Ibid.*

The Trust of Children

The faith of a child is more precisely described as trust or confidence. "What is trustworthy?" a child may be asked. "My parents are trustworthy," she answers, "and so are my teachers and my church. My world is trustworthy." That is a seven-year-old speaking.

I felt a tinge of guilt the other day, as all parents must when childhood faith is invaded. Brian and I were reading a book that told of a burglar breaking into a family's home, and I happened to mention that a home we lived in once had been robbed. I didn't think about the conversation again. But for the next week my son returned again and again to that story. "How did the burglar get into our house? Why didn't you stop him? Why do burglars break into people's houses?" After I explained to him that the burglar had stolen our television set, he responded, "Why didn't he use his own money to buy a TV?"

When not afflicted with the adult experience, children believe that life is inherently fair. They believe in reward and punishment and that "the good guys" always win. They believe that they will be protected from harm. Children need to believe these things, and the childhood years can be cruel when the ambiguity comes crashing in around them too soon. Yet, the reality is that not even a child can afford to believe for long that everyone in every situation will be fair or that everyone is worthy of trust. If only in a small way, when you teach children not to talk to strangers, you encroach upon their innocence. When the myths of childhood are broken (for example, in our culture — Santa Claus, the Easter bunny, or the tooth fairy), innocence is invaded.

Cracks in a Solid Wall

In reality childhood is like a solid wall of simple trust and unshaken confidence. How natural it would be to hear a child defiantly face a truthful accusation with, "My daddy would never do that!" when in fact her daddy did do it and all the evidence, as well as her daddy's own admission, points to the same reality.

As a child approaches adolescence, cracks begin to appear in the solid wall. "What is trustworthy?" you ask a teenager. "My parents aren't. My old man cheats on his taxes, and my mom drinks too much when she thinks I'm not watching."

"What's trustworthy?" you ask a teenager. "The church isn't. Most of those folks say one thing on Sunday morning and act just like everyone else through the week."

"What's trustworthy?" you ask a teenager. "My body isn't trustworthy anymore. My voice squeaks at the most embarrassing moments. I get crazy feelings inside for a special person who doesn't even know that I exist. My mind wanders, and I can't seem to keep it on track. I can't even sit still when I want to 'cause my body seems to be in constant motion. I feel like my feelings are on a roller coaster. I jerk from one intense feeling to another without knowing how or why."

Cracks appear in what was once a solid wall. Welcome to adolescence! Welcome to ambiguity! The teen question is "Now that you know there are situations and realities that don't and won't make sense, what are you going to do about it?"

There are plenty of negative responses to that question among today's adolescents. The suicide rate is at its highest level in these years. Many teenage girls become pregnant, thinking that having babies to love will patch up the cracks in the wall. Alcohol and drug addiction divert young persons from the ambiguity of crumbled childhood walls.

There are youth for whom the recognition of limits and ambiguity hits like a cold shower in January, while for others it's more like a cold shower in July. There is no reasonable explanation for such different responses. Yet, it is undoubtedly more difficult for youth to face life's ambiguities when the adults around them live with their own diversions.

I can recall the cracks that first appeared in my childhood wall. During seventh grade I worked in a grocery store. A part-time pastor also worked there. One day the two of us were stocking shelves after the delivery truck arrived. He handed me a box of feminine hygiene products to unload, and as we were putting them on the shelf, I asked him what they were. He responded, "You don't know?" I lamely responded, "Oh, yeah," pretending that I knew, but by that time he was halfway back to the storeroom where gales of laughter were soon heard from the rest of the staff. Because of that incident, I lost all respect for the man, refusing to accept the fact that a pastor, like anyone else, can make mistakes. I was not able to realize that when asked an embarrassing question, a pastor can turn to mockery just as easily as any other human being.

There were a number of couples in my childhood church who were my parents' age, and all were important role models for me. Today they are people whom I deeply respect and admire, but they did not always live up to my naive childlike expectations. When I was in seventh grade, one couple chaperoned our youth group. To our shock, one evening they gave in to our insistent requests and allowed us to play the game Spin the Bottle in the church basement. The husband went around the church building, making sure no other adults were in sight before we began to play. I heard him whisper to his wife, "I sure hope the preacher doesn't come to church tonight." She responded, "Oh, he won't. He's gone to Springfield." The youth never talked about it after that night because each one of us suspected there was something very wrong with what we did. Adults were never to be trusted in quite the same way.

Later, when I was to enter senior high school, our Sunday church school teacher was very popular with the youth. His class was always crowded with youth who appreciated the questions that he allowed and the free-wheeling discussion that often veered away from "the quarterlies" (the curriculum books). One of the important role-model couples got wind of the unorthodox approach of this teacher and used their influence to have him dismissed. The teacher left the church at the beginning of the fall when I was to enter his class. Some months later when my older sister told me the whole story, a huge crack broke open for me. For the first time adults appeared more defensive and less trustworthy, as if they had something to hide that my questions might uncover.

Today I give thanks for each of those experiences (and many more) because they broke down the innocence and naiveté of my childhood walls. Children assume that adults don't err, that they don't waiver, that they don't despair, that the aren't uncertain, and that they aren't hypocritical. And when the "warts" begin to appear on important role models, the reality of adolescence comes crashing in.

What Is Faith?

Faith is not dogma, not doctrine, not religion, and not belief. *Faith is a stance that is necessitated because human experience is inherently ambiguous.* Faith can either address the ambiguity or sidestep it. The first is healthy; the second, destructive.

The more profoundly one questions the assumptions of childhood, the deeper one feels the ambiguity. Profound adult faith feels the ambiguity more deeply than superficial adult faith.

Faith and certainty are not synonymous. The more certain I am of something, the less faith is required to believe in its truth. Yet *there is a correlation between certainty and trust.* If I am absolutely certain of something, I trust in it. Faith is not as necessary when you know something beyond a shadow of a doubt. Only in doubt's shadows is faith crucial.

There is a correlation between uncertainty and faith. Little or no faith is required to believe that you are now reading this book. More faith is required to believe *in* this book.

If you have no questions about God, no uncertainty or doubt, then you have little need for faith in God. It is only when you consider that you cannot prove God's existence to yourself or to others, or that you may not understand God's will for your life, that faith is essential. "Now faith is the assurance of things hoped for, the conviction of things not seen" (Hebrews 11:1). We have faith in that which we cannot see, which we cannot know, which we cannot prove.

In the face of ambiguity, I have faith. I believe in the New Testament as an authoritative resource for faith. I recognize that it could be a cruel hoax, and I can offer little to prove it otherwise. But I choose not to believe that it is a hoax. I choose to put my faith in the stories of Jesus' life, death, and resurrection, even though I can prove none of them.

Yet, it is possible to be confident in faith. In fact, faith offers confidence in light of what we cannot know or control. Faith offers an alternative to meaninglessness. In spite of the fact that I cannot prove that Jesus lived, died, or was resurrected, my faith in those events gives me confidence to live with thanksgiving and joy. Take away that faith, and I am left with regret and despair. I have walked the Christian pilgrimage long enough to have some confidence that if I trust in God's way, my way will be better. Yet, I cannot prove this, and when I'm honest, there remain many times when I lack confidence myself.

Ambiguity and Faith—Universal Experiences

Ambiguity is universal. The longer you live, the more likely you respect the ambiguity. Cocksure graduates from the university later admit that much of what they "knew" must now be accepted on faith. Minor-league physicists "know" a lot more than those on the cutting edge of research. The ambiguity revolves not only around religious issues but also in the area of science. Science is built upon theories, not facts, and scientific insight is possible only if you have faith in those theories.

Love has ambiguities. Why is it that those whom we love the most also hurt us the most? Teenagers know about that. Marriage has its ambiguities. I haven't stood with nearly one hundred grooms awaiting their weddings without gaining a deep appreciation for the ambiguity of marriage. Churches are also ambiguous places. Although they are full of selfishness and grudges, we call them "God's redemptive communities." Try to make sense of that at sixteen years of age! Is God deceived? Does not God know what "God's People" are up to?

Ambiguity is universal. No one can entirely escape it. While some teenagers live in protected environments and may postpone it, none will completely escape an encounter with the ambiguity of life. The daughter of a wealthy family who has been given every privilege and opportunity cannot understand why her younger brother was born retarded. It doesn't make sense. It cannot be resolved.

Debbie's father was devout and took Debbie and her older brother to church while her mother stayed at home. From an early age Debbie was deeply impressed by her father's commitment to their church and his disciplines of daily prayer and Bible study. Debbie also assumed that her church was a loving Christian fellowship and thought of it as a second home throughout her childhood years. This attitude continued until her father was treated unfairly by another church member when Debbie was just beginning high school. At about the same time Debbie brought a Jewish friend to her church's youth group, and the other youth told "Jewish jokes" behind her back. Debbie was so disillusioned that she turned away from the church and Christianity, which, in her words, "broke my father's heart." She attended a synagogue with a boyfriend throughout the remainder of her high school years and experimented with Buddhism in college. Later she characterized those years as a time of running away from something that did not make sense to her—"a religion of love that could be so cruel."

Some teenagers try hard to make the childhood confidences work. They do everything right; they play by the rules; they try harder than anyone else; they believe that life can be conquered or that whatever they want can be theirs if they are good enough or work hard enough. But if they cannot recognize the ambiguity in their lives, it is only because they are running so hard in the opposite direction. Just wait. Follow these young people and watch what happens when they first get cheated out of what they feel they've rightfully earned. When the "bubble" breaks, and it will, so will a faith that believes that "everyone wins who plays by the rules."

Many young people will find diversions from the ambiguity. Sexual or drug exploitation, money, or material comforts can serve as diversions, and a faith stance can be developed around these things (Matthew 6:24-26).

If we can affirm that the ambiguity of life is universal, and if we choose to affirm that life is God's gift, then in some way we must reconcile faith in such a way that it addresses rather than avoids the ambiguity. Mature faith in God can make the ambiguity more tolerable; it can reduce its poignancy or pain; it can help us trust in its ultimate resolution; it can make the ambiguity less bothersome. But healthy faith never fully denies that life has unanswered questions.

If God had wanted to give us life devoid of ambiguity, life without choice, without variety, without difficulty, without questions, without uncertainty, then God surely could have done so. But God did not choose this gift. The gift God chooses to give us requires faith to receive.

Therefore, *faith is universal.* Everyone is in need of some response to the ambiguities first encountered as an adolescent. Everyone searches for meaning in the face of meaninglessness. No one escapes faith! No one is "faith-less."

Adolescents and the Shaping of Faith

Adolescence is the important moment in the life span to shape a personal faith because it is typically the first time to encounter fully life's ambiguities. That is not to imply that faith is shaped in adolescence and untouched throughout adulthood, but the shaping is usually more dynamic and surely more foundational in adolescence.

The need for faith is lifelong, though for most people the need takes on a decidedly more intense pace during adolescence. The beginning foundations laid during the teen years are often outgrown, but they do have a lifelong impact. The term "faith shaping" as used in this book refers to the intensity during the adolescent years of forming a faith stance in response to one's early encounters with life's ambiguities.

Underneath, if not on the surface, young persons are pleading for help in facing the ambiguities they have encountered. They want help in facing the nagging and unanswered questions about their life situation and their future. If faith is life's foundation, then we had best help youth build it before we worry a great deal about the appearance of the structure. "The greater the building that has to be errected, the greater the need that the foundation be good. Religion is the most inclusive and most far reaching aspect of life, and requires adequate foundations."[3]

Life Is Biased

Some adults are deceived into believing that youth need a neutral environment of faith in which to grow up. Perhaps those adults felt their freedom limited or violated during their adolescent years and now overcompensate in their response to teenagers.

I remember meeting a woman who boldly espoused a philosophy of

[3]R. S. Lee, *Your Growing Child and Religion* (New York: Macmillan Publishing Company, 1963), p. 15.

intending to raise her children in an unbiased faith orientation. She had decided that faith was only an adult affair and that she would not influence her children one way or another. When I visited in her home, I observed that she had consciously left out a Christian perspective in her childrearing. But it did not take long to realize that instead of a Christian faith, she was modeling a faith that prized an academic, scientific world view that, in fact, matched her own faith commitments, and her children were deeply steeped in that faith bias.

The naiveté of such an adult is in thinking that a neutral faith environment is possible. It is surely possible to raise a child with no mention of Christ, nor of Baptists, nor of liberal Christianity. But it is not possible to raise children and adolescents in an unbiased faith environment.

Life is biased! One of the ways in which the ambiguity of life comes crashing in on some youth is when they question the home in which they were raised: Why were my parents rich or poor? black or white? American or Filipino? living in the Northern or Southern Hemisphere? Why are some children born in a land of malnutrition and others into a land of plenty? Why are some children conceived in the wombs of mothers who are neither prepared to provide the love and discipline that the children will need nor mature enough to recognize that fact? Why are some children born with mental or physical handicaps? Why? It isn't fair. The advantages and/or disadvantages of parents, home, and heritage begin life's bias. The moment we speak one language to a child, life is biased. When we chose one value over another, life is biased.

The bias is what makes life human. Most of the good things about our lives are derived from the richness of family and cultural bias. Every parent, civilization, church, and race nurtures a faith bias in subtle, unconscious ways throughout the life of the young person.

That is not to claim that every bias is good or healthy. Prejudice is an obviously distorted bias. We constantly need to reshape our biases in more mature ways. Martin Luther King, Jr., once said, "Softmindedness is one of the basic causes of race prejudice. The toughminded person always examines the facts before he reaches conclusions; in short, he postjudges. The tenderminded person reaches a conclusion before he has examined the first fact; in short, he prejudges and is prejudiced."[4]

It is naive to believe that the important persons in a teenager's life should never advocate their own values. That is as silly as to claim that

[4]Martin Luther King, Jr., *Strength to Love* (New York: Harper & Row, Publishers Inc., 1963), p. 4.

one value is as good as another or that it doesn't matter what you believe just as long as you believe in something. There are negative and destructive values just as there are positive and life-giving values.

A Conscious Effort

Since children and youth cannot escape our faith bias, then why must faith be nurtured by conscious effort? Why can't it simply happen? Yet, if we care about the depth, the health, and the very stance of faith that adolescents will shape, then our nurture must be a conscious effort.

The outward manifestations of adults' bias of faith might be obvious to children, but the inward motivation is often not obvious. Faith is foundational, and it must be lifted up in order to be seen and understood. I have known many parents who have failed to lift up the foundations of their faith, and their children grew up unaware of its depth or meaning.

No adult lives up to the faith that he or she professes. We are all sporadic and occasional in our faithfulness. If we do not consciously nurture faith, we send confusing signals of word and deed. By nurturing in an honest, confessional spirit, we assist adolescents in the faith-shaping journey.

Finally, we nurture faith with adolescents not only because they need to be aware of our faith bias but also because through nurture we can assist them in the shaping of their own faith. Through nurture we can raise the right questions and help youth be in touch with appropriate resources as they address life's ambiguities rather than avoid them.

For these reasons, it is imperative that adolescents be surrounded by adults who take seriously the call to nurture faith.

2

Nurture and Transformation

Nurture in the Christian context occurs whenever we are made more ready for a transforming encounter with the Transcendent. Formation opens us up to transformation.

NURTURE: formation that leads or opens us to transformation or conversion; the work of God or of a faith community

TRANSFORMATION: God's unique work in the world, the change from old to new

EVANGELISM: the church's call to transformation (or conversion)

CONVERSION PROCESS: the process whereby we experience God's transforming presence throughout our lives

There are many confusing assumptions about the roles of nurture and transformation in the Christian life. There is an assumption, evident in much of the church's thinking today, that nurture exists for its own sake. Who would argue that young people need to be nurtured by adults? But nurture is not an end in itself, but rather a means toward an end. Toward what purpose are we nurturing adolescents? One probable response is that we are nurturing adolescents to become mature Christians. But is that possible? Can we nurture young persons to "become Christians"? Or is that out of our hands? Or, for that matter, is that out of their hands as well?

If we are called to nurture youth as they shape their faith, then it is imperative that we understand the reason for Christian nurture.

John Westerhoff has written,

Christians are not born. Neither are they simply made, formed or nurtured. Conversion—a reorientation of life, a change of heart, mind and behavior—is a necessary aspect of mature Christian faith whether one grows up in the church or not. The church can no longer maintain the illusion that child nurture in and of itself can or will kindle the fire of Christian faith either in particular persons or in the church as a whole.[1]

Westerhoff is correct in maintaining that Christians are neither born nor nurtured. Becoming a Christian is not a slow, unintentional process of evolution in which a young person eventually "ends up as a Christian." The Christian call is for "metanoia," a Greek New Testament word which means to change one's way of being. It calls for revolutionary not evolutionary change. Jesus came to his ministry calling for radical repentance (Mark 1:15). We "become" Christians by a radical transformation of our lives, turnaround experiences that must not happen just once but many times.

Stating this, I don't wish to question those who cannot identify the point at which they made their first "profession of faith." It would be hard to imagine anyone raised in a more faith-oriented environment than myself. My parents are both articulate spokespersons of faith and active leaders in their church. Nearly all of my family's friends during my childhood years were also active church members. We spent many hours each week at the church. If anyone could have "evolved" into Christian faith, I qualified. And for that reason I have difficulty identifying my "first" decision of faith, or when I actually chose Christianity for myself. I can identify, at nine years of age, when I decided to share with my church an early faith decision.

But at issue here is not a time line of the decisions of faith we have made but rather the *transformations*. Decisions are "our work," but there is no way for the church to transform persons and no way for us to transform ourselves. When we attempt this, we place ourselves in the role of God. God alone is the transforming power in the universe.

It is possible for us to *reform*, to go back to an earlier form. It is possible for us to *conform*, to make ourselves like another desirable form. It is possible for us to *deform* something, to take away its form, or attempt to be *uniform*, to appear in the same shape or form as others.

But transformation is qualitatively different. Transformation involves the change from old form to new form, from an "old me" to a "new me." When that occurs in human experience, it is God's doing. We are not gifted with that ability. Bonhoeffer has written, "Here stands Christ, in the centre, between me and myself, between the old existence and the new."[2]

---

[1]John H. Westerhoff, *Inner Growth—Outer Change: An Educational Guide to Church Renewal* (New York: Seabury Press, 1979), p. 21.

[2]Dietrich Bonhoeffer, *Christ the Centre* (New York: Harper & Row, Publishers, Inc., 1966), p. 61.

Paul wrote to the Galatians, ". . . I feel the same kind of pain for you until Christ's nature is *formed* in you." (Galatians 4:19, TEV, my emphasis). Throughout Paul's writing, he discussed in analagous terms the form of Christ that is to be embodied within us (Colossians 3:9-10; Galatians 2:20 and 3:27; 2 Corinthians 5:17; Ephesians 4:22-24). Bonhoeffer wrote,

> To be conformed to the image of Christ is not an ideal to be striven after. It is not as though we had to imitate him as well as we could. We cannot transform ourselves into his image; it is rather *the form of Christ which seeks to be formed in us* (Galatians 4:19), and to be manifested in us. Christ's work in us is not finished until he has perfected his own form in us[3] (emphasis added by author).

God's work in the world and in our lives is transformational. We cannot control nor predict when or how it will break into our lives or into society. We can, of course, close ourselves off from it, or we can make ourselves more open to God's transforming moments.

Nurture in the Christian context occurs whenever we are made more ready for a transforming encounter with the Transcendent. Formation opens us up to transformation. Westerhoff said, "We can nurture persons into institutional religion, but not mature Christian faith. We do not gradually educate persons to be mature Christians."[4] Here Westerhoff is incorrect to suggest that the purpose of nurture is necessarily to advance institutional religion. That is not the intended purpose of Christian nurture. Unless nurture opens persons to God's transforming work, it is something less than Christian nurture.

Nurture then is the work of the church; it is communal in character. It makes little sense to speak of nurturing ourselves. Others nurture us and we nurture others. It is interactive.

It is my belief, though it cannot be verified, that transformation never occurs unless we have first been nurtured toward the encounter, however unconscious that may have been. Nurture is not exclusively a human task, for God also nurtures. It may be that God has nurtured someone to the point of readiness, separate from or in company with the human nurture of the church or home.

Even though nurture can occur spontaneously, as we pointed out in the conclusion of chapter one, nurture also needs to be intentional. *Inten-*

---

[3]Dietrich Bonhoeffer, *The Cost of Discipleship* (New York: Macmillan Publishing Company, 1963), p. 341.
[4]Westerhoff, p. 21.

tional nurture is another name for *Christian education.* Christian education is interested in biblical literacy or theological inquiry only so far as they prepare persons to encounter God in Christ. (Religious education is more scholarly in focus and less concerned with nurture. It would be legitimately interested in biblical literacy or theological inquiry as ends in themselves without necessarily leading to transformation.) The goal of intentional Christian nurture is not the acquisition of facts or the development of expertise but learning a style of openness, receptivity, prayer, discernment, risk, and response.

There is such a thing, then as *Christian learning*, and it is the result of Christian nurture. It is best described by Jesus: "Take my yoke upon you, and learn from me . . . " (Matthew 11:29). It is the opposite of the more secular style of learning characterized in John 7:15: "The Jews marveled at it, saying, 'How is it that this man has learning, when he has never studied?' " It is the difference between learning *about* and learning *of.* The goal of Christian learning is preparation for a transforming encounter with God in Christ. Often when we have thought we were nurturing youth in the faith, we were only offering them information about Christianity rather than preparing them for this transforming encounter.

Evangelism and Transformation

In light of what we have said about nurture and transformation, we can now define evangelism. Like nurture, evangelism is the church's task (though God also evangelizes). *Evangelism is the call to transformation.* Nurture provides the fertile climate in which evangelism can be proclaimed.

Transformation, or conversion, is not what we in the church have thought it to be. Westerhoff says,

> Conversion implies the reordering of our perceptions, a radical change without which no further growth or learning is possible. Conversion therefore is not an end, but a new beginning. . . . Conversion is not to be understood only in the sense of a shift from no faith to another faith to Christian faith; it is also an essential dimension in the life of all baptized, faithful Christians.[5]

Our preoccupation with evangelism as a call to a one-time decision of faith has mistakenly led many youth to feel that they have "graduated" from faith as they walk away from the waters of baptism or the service of confirmation. We have posed the evangelistic question as, "Either you are a Christian, or you are not."

[5]Ibid, pp. 21-22.

The problem with this one-time orientation is that even though I long ago made my first-time profession of faith in Christ as my Lord and Savior, and then as Lord and Savior of the world, I still am not fully transformed. Why? Because at the time, and at every time since then, I have given only a part, and God asks for a whole. Paul was correct when he wrote, "Therefore, if any one is in Christ, he is a new creation; the old has passed away, behold, the new has come" (2 Corinthians 5:17). But Christ awaits my willingness to be fully united.

I withhold . . . Christ waits . . . the church evangelizes (calls) . . . and God seeks to fully transform the "old" to the "new." And until I fully repent, Christ cannot fully transform, and I am not fully evangelized.

Evangelism is not a call to a one-time decision but to a first-time decision of faith that leads to many more decisions of faith. The evangelistic question is not "How many Christians are there?" That is a statistician's question. The evangelistic question is "Are persons being transformed in Christ?"

When we think of evangelism with youth, we normally think of those who have yet to make first-time decisions, the "un-reached," but we also need to consider the ongoing evangelistic call to those reaching for the fulness of Christ in their lives. All young people need to be evangelized until they can claim with Paul, ". . . It is no longer I who live, but it is Christ who lives in me" (Galatians 2:20, TEV). And with Paul again, we must help young people recognize,

> I do not claim that I have already succeeded or have already become perfect. I keep striving to win the prize for which Christ Jesus has already won me to himself. Of course, my brothers, I really do not think that I have already won it; the one thing I do, however, is to forget what is behind me and do my best to reach what is ahead. So I run straight toward the goal in order to win the prize, which is God's call through Christ Jesus to the life above" (Philippians 3:12-14, TEV).

Thomas Merton has said, "We are not converted only once in our lives, but many times; and this endless series of large and small conversions, inner revolutions, leads to our transformation in Christ."[6]

Many junior high youth are developmentally able to make a first profession of faith, and the church should affirm them as they do so. The church's formal affirmation of that decision is the act of baptism or confirmation. Most junior high youth are not, however, mature enough to

---

[6]Thomas Merton, in a letter published in *Information Catholiques Internationale*, April 1973, back cover.

make one-time decisions of any kind. The junior high faith decision is primarily a directional one, and they are well served when this is interpreted to them.

If transformation or conversion is a process rather than an event, if it reoccurs throughout one's lifetime, then we might ask if the process has a recurring pattern. Can a sequential process for transformation be described? I believe that in general we can describe the process, though much depends upon circumstance, personality, and individual decision-making styles.

The Transformation Process

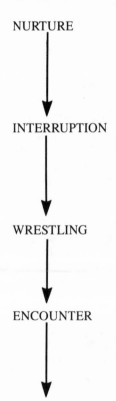

NURTURE

At normal seasons of my life I am subject to nurture by God or by the intentional as well as spontaneous nurture of God's community of faith. Unconsciously or consciously, I learn styles of openness, receptivity, and prayer and develop gifts of discernment and risk taking.

INTERRUPTION

The Spirit's interruption is rarely anticipated. Sometimes its presence is disturbing and unwanted. I always feel stirred, upset, challenged, or made uncomfortable by the Spirit's interruption. This can come through some event, person, idea, or vision.

WRESTLING

The nurture I have received may determine whether this stage is a brief pause or long struggle. I may fight off the Spirit's interruption as a nuisance, a troubling presence, or a disturbing call.

ENCOUNTER

When I finally relent, I say, "I'm ready now. Come in, Spirit of God." Often I may experience a great or sudden openness to transformation. A word may be encountered as if hearing it for the very first time, or a vision received, or a call perceived. This is often intuitive; I can't yet describe or explain my experience of this encounter. For youth this is most often an emotional experience.

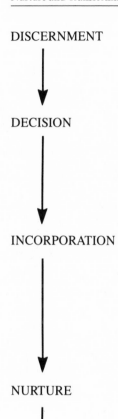

DISCERNMENT

The call now becomes more definite as I seek to understand the encounter. I ask, "What does this transformation mean? How can I describe it? What sense can I make of it?" Often discernment arises from dialogue with another person.

DECISION

Transformation usually leaves me with a choice. God has shown me a way, a vision, a direction, or a call. As I discern its meaning, I recognize that I have a decision to make. "Yes" or "No"—What is my response? By this time the decision can appear costly and difficult or exciting and compelling.

INCORPORATION

Reality is now shifting as I choose to incorporate the transformation that God has introduced to my existing lifestyle. I must now get acquainted with the "new me." I must gain a new sense of who I am in relation to who it is that God is calling me to become. This may involve compromise and realism. I have given "some" but not "all." It is this process of incorporation that demands that I again experience transformation.

NURTURE

Life again has returned to a more normal time. I may be relieved, discouraged, or excited, but life goes on, as does the nurture by God and by God's community of faith. I have experienced transformation and must again learn new styles of prayer and receptivity. And the process reoccurs over and over.

The Process of Transformation

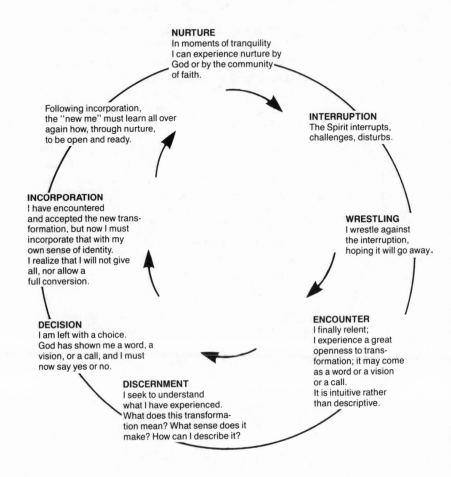

NURTURE
In moments of tranquility
I can experience nurture by
God or by the community
of faith.

INTERRUPTION
The Spirit interrupts,
challenges, disturbs.

Following incorporation,
the "new me" must learn all over
again how, through nurture,
to be open and ready.

WRESTLING
I wrestle against
the interruption,
hoping it will go away.

INCORPORATION
I have encountered
and accepted the new transformation, but now I must
incorporate that with my
own sense of identity.
I realize that I will not give
all, nor allow a
full conversion.

ENCOUNTER
I finally relent;
I experience a great
openness to trans-
formation; it may come
as a word or a vision
or a call.
It is intuitive rather
than descriptive.

DECISION
I am left with a choice.
God has shown me a word, a
vision, or a call, and I must
now say yes or no.

DISCERNMENT
I seek to understand
what I have experienced.
What does this transformation mean? What sense does it
make? How can I describe it?

If the transformation process suggests anything close to reality, it must be clear why transformations are such victories in anyone's life, particularly for adolescents. At any point in the sequence, persons can and do retreat from the process, thwarting real transformation. Persons may linger for days, months, or years at one particular point. Youth will encounter the transformation process by trial and error. Fortunately, youth tend to be risk takers with less to lose than adults whose lifestyles call for more caution.

However, we also need to be aware that many youth in the faith-shaping process may breeze through the first stages of this process, as in a mountaintop experience, only to find the incorporation (the going back home) all the more painful and difficult. At that point they may feel that because they have given "some" but not "all" that they have failed or that God is unable to truly transform.

Now it becomes more clear that what we have tended to do with adolescents is to emphasize primarily the decision phase in the transformation sequence (which is coincidentally the phase most in our own control) and to de-emphasize those phases instigated by God (nurture, interruption, encounter) and to disavow those phases where we find ourselves in tension with God (wrestling, incorporation).

Perhaps the only effective way to nurture youth through the process of transformation is for them to witness adults within the same process. Our fears and joys as we encounter the God who transforms may be the best invitation to them to become receptive to the evangelistic call.

Short-Sighted Nurture

When churches consider the nurture of faith with adolescents, the assumption is that the focus is upon preparation for baptism and church membership or confirmation. Adults respond as though youth are making a one-time decision of faith. Many churches use one or more of these misdirected approaches as their only focused nurture of faith with adolescents:

The Aisle Approach

The altar call is the only way to respond to the faith needs of youth. Get each of them to make the conversion decision. Once they are saved, the important work is done. Let's get our youth walking down the aisle.

The Batch Approach

A faith decision is embarrassing to young people when they are singled out, so we take a group of them at a time, have them sit with the pastor during Lent, and baptize/confirm them all on Palm Sunday.

The Osmosis Approach

We don't make any conscious effort with our youth in terms of the nurture of their faith. We believe that by example, faith will rub off naturally. Faith is contagious!

The Busybody Approach

Keep the youth busy! Fill all their time with church activities, and they won't have the chance to consider other alternatives. They'll become strong, active Christians.

The Rob-the-Cradle Approach

Get to the children because they are more impressionable. The adolescents are too reluctant and embarrassed to make decisions of faith, and they already have questions and doubts. It never hurt any child to make a commitment of faith.

The Institutional Approach

We stress membership in the church, not relationship to God in Christ. Faith is just too illusive for most young people to understand. They can relate to the tangible demands of belonging to the church.

Actually, our shortsightedness in the way we nurture faith with youth is probably reflective of our own bewilderment in our role as nurturers of faith. There is a great deal of insecurity and fear whenever most adults talk with youth about their faith. Likely this is why most of these encounters are reserved for pastors, though as a pastor I admit to my own fears and insecurities.

There are many legitimate questions: How strongly should I advocate my faith with youth? If I feel uncertain with my own faith, should I hide this from youth who have enough uncertainties of their own? When should youth make decisions of faith? Should children be allowed to make them? Shouldn't lifelong decisions of any kind be postponed until the young adult years? How do I overcome my personal embarrassment in discussing matters of faith with youth? Is it possible to teach faith? Isn't it caught rather than taught? How do we nurture faith with youth in an age in which there are so many competing value systems available to them? Why are our youth in the church often more enculturated into those other value systems?

Overcoming the Problems

We desire to nurture a faith with adolescents that truly addresses life's inherent ambiguities. The cracks that appear in childhood's walls demand a response of adolescents. Without our caring nurture, faith will likely become a diversion from the ambiguity. Through nurture, we will not be trying to force young people to make faith decisions. Rather, we will be trying to assist them as they learn ways to become open to God's transforming presence. As evangelists, we will be sensitively extending the call time and again, to youth and to ourselves, to be ready and open for the transformations God has in mind for us.

At one point Jesus' disciples were attempting to assert their own power over one another. As they walked to Capernaum, they were trying to decide who was first among them. When they arrived, Jesus pulled them aside saying, "Whoever wants to be first must place himself last. . . ." Then he took a nearby child and putting his arms around the child, Jesus said to the disciples, "Whoever welcomes in my name one of these children, welcomes me; and whoever welcomes me, welcomes not only me but also the one who sent me" (Mark 9:35-37, TEV).

Our task as adults is to welcome children and youth into the loving reality of God's reign on earth. Ours is not to push or force or avoid, but to welcome. Whoever opens the door of faith to one of these welcomes not only that young person but also the God of heaven and earth.

3

Two Nurturing Behaviors

F*aith advocacy and faith clarification are important behaviors for those adults who care to nurture adolescents in their faith pilgrimage. Without resourceful adults who are willing to stand in these roles, our efforts in welcoming youth into the faith will lack integrity and effectiveness.*

FAITH CLARIFICATION: a behavior attempting to help young persons clarify their faith questions

FAITH ADVOCACY: a behavior attempting to bring the faith nearly or directly to young persons

NEARNESS: bringing faithful activities and traditions near to youth

DIRECTNESS: presenting the claims of faith directly to young persons in an open and appealing way

We can identify two nurturing behaviors for adults desiring to assist youth who seek to shape a more personal faith in the face of life's ambiguities. In so doing, adults will need to learn effective, noncoercive ways to *advocate* faith and *clarify* faith. Both are nurturing behaviors.

Adults Who Advocate Faith

There are two ways to advocate faith with youth: by nearness and by directness.

Nearness

Nurture requires that there must be a nearness (closeness) to the faithful community and its traditions, rituals, and stories. *Being near to faith and its traditions is pivotal to effective nurture with youth.*

If traditions of faith rarely enter the home, then faith is not near. If the stories of faith are heard only through occasional or casual church attend-ance and nothing more, then faith is not near.

The faith is near when adults live out their faith in natural but expressive ways before the young person. The faith is near when the young person feels that he or she is an integral part of the church. The faith is near when the young person is allowed to develop deep relationships with adult Christian models. The faith is near when families are not embarrassed to express faith and when parents verbalize their commitments. The faith is near when families develop and practice faithful traditions and rituals in the home. The faith is near when youth see how much faith is prized by the important adults around them.

Nothing brings the faith nearer to youth than the way in which their parents prize their own faith and relationship with the church. If faith is of great importance, then the child will be brought near to it. If not, the child will likely feel more distance from it.

For effective nurture, the home and the church must be in harmony in bringing faith near to young people. Parents and churches who change their priorities midstream, allowing new priorities to be expressed, can have an impact in imparting faith to children. Often parents or church leaders claim a very profound personal faith but are casual in the way they express this to their children. Children often observe this and are impressed by the discrepancy.

Many parents are deceived about how near they bring the faith to their children and youth. The assertions "I took my child to church every Sunday," "I served on a committee down there for a while," or "We prayed before every meal in our home" might be indicative of the misunderstanding. If these things are done out of compulsion or obligation, or done with little investment, then faith will not be brought near to those young people.

Churches have their own deceptions about how nearly faith is brought to youth. If churches plan activities as if youth are a specialized compartment of the church, then the youth themselves will not feel valued or included in congregational fellowship, and nearness will not be encouraged. Or if a church's ministry with youth is designed merely to keep them busy, but in fact does not develop its own rituals and traditions of faith and trust, then nearness is not encouraged. Finally, if churches approach youth ministry using only artificial clichés that are not experientially linked to the lives of youth, faith will not be brought near.

The New Testament speaks mainly of first-generation adult Christians, so it is difficult to cite an example of nearness from its pages. Paul, however, in his second letter to Timothy did speak of nearness in Timothy's upbringing. Timothy was as close to Paul as a son would be to a father. Paul spoke of him in 2 Timothy 1:2-3 as "my beloved child . . .[whom] I remember . . . constantly in my prayers." Paul was an important role model for this young man. In 2 Timothy 1:5, Paul said, "I am reminded of your sincere faith, a faith that dwelt first in your grandmother Lois and your mother Eunice and now, I am sure, dwells in you."

Timothy was a third-generation Christian and had a heritage of faith from his grandmother and mother. It appeared evident that Timothy had been raised as a youth near to the church, near to its faithful traditions, near to a home where faith was prized and enjoyed, near to important adult Christian models, and near to a whole community of friends who did not fear to speak of their commitments in the face of adversity.

Paul used this reminder of the nearness of faith in Timothy's younger years to encourage him to persevere and to accept his share of suffering. Paul said that it was the nearness that would be an anchor to him during this time.

Directness

There must be specific times when the issues of faith are presented directly to young persons. In some churches and homes we are embarrassed to bring our concerns about faith to this point. It may be that we feel insecure to be able to answer with precision all questions that youth may raise. And often churches and parents are so overreactive against coercive or manipulative approaches that they err on the side of neglect.

Directness is presenting the desire of God to transform a young person. This is done in an appealing, fair, and open way. It is not pressuring young people or forcing decisions. Indeed, directness focuses upon a decision of faith as only one aspect of the process of transformation. It also directly advocates with young people to be open and receptive to God's transformational invitation and legitimizes those moments when young people find themselves in struggle or tension as a result of transforming encounters with God.

The way that we directly offer faith to a young person needs to occur in relation to a teenager's maturity, life experience, and interest. It happens on God's developmental timetable, and not our own. Youth are not statistics, nor is faith quantitative.

Directness occurs when we intentionally assist young persons in writing new chapters in their faith stories. Directness occurs when we share our own faith story and faith bias. Directness implies searching discussions with youth about the meaning of their personal faith. Directness

includes occasions when worship is intimate, when prayer touches reality, and when servanthood is suddenly eye-opening. Directness happens
when we help youth address their own questions of faith. Directness
occurs when we share our own faith story and faith bias. Directness
occurs whenever we give shape and focus to those moments when youth
appear ready to open themselves more fully to God.

There are many examples when Jesus sensed the readiness of those
around him and presented the claims of faith directly to them. Perhaps the
earliest example in the Gospels is the calling of the disciples. Jesus must
have sensed their readiness for transformation as he extended God's call:
"Follow me . . ." (Matthew 4:19).

Nearness and Directness Together

Nearness and directness are complementary nurturing behaviors in
advocating faith with youth. Faith can be advocated nearly to children
from the moment of birth. Faith is advocated directly to older children
and adolescents in response to their inquiries and questions. This will
occur with more frequency in the teen years. And for those persons who
do not face the ambiguities of life until after the teen years, directness may
be offered but will not be heard.

Two examples of nearness and directness in the lives of young people
might prove helpful.

A young girl named Janet came with a friend to the youth group of the
church that I was pastoring. Although Janet came from an unchurched
family, it wasn't long before she became a full participant in all facets of
our youth ministry. During a church musical she played a leading role. In
a relatively brief time, from the church's perspective, we had developed a
significant pattern of nearness with Janet. As time passed, Janet and I had
occasional and brief conversations about her faith. She was able to
express doubts about whether "a friendly God" existed. One time,
returning from a youth retreat, we were sitting together in front of the
church bus while many other youth were sleeping. As I drove down out of
the mountains, Janet and I discussed openly and searchingly her own
relationship with God and the issue of her acceptance of God's love. She
made no immediate response following our conversation, but it was an
opportunity for directness. I have no idea whether Janet ever accepted the
transforming love of Jesus Christ. But that is not my responsibility. My
responsibility was to be a member of a team of adults who would bring
faith nearly and directly to her.

Jack was a young person who came from an articulate family. Both of his parents were expressive about their faith. They had both been church school teachers for adults and youth. Jack was their oldest child. He grew up as an active participant in the church, and it was an important support community for him. The faith was brought both nearly and directly to him through the church and his home. Halfway through his senior year, without any apparent reason, Jack needed distance and personal space, so he rebelled against the church and against his faith heritage. Ten months later the rebellion ceased. Throughout this separation his church and parents expressed loving concern—but no coercion. As Jack moved back into the fellowship of the church, he returned with more personal issues. Our responsibility was to bring the faith to him nearly and directly, allowing him his own responses.

Adults Who Clarify Faith

As well as being advocates of faith, adult nurturers need to assist in clarifying issues of faith as youth confront the ambiguities of life. Rather than providing answers, the faith clarifier raises questions that can point the young person toward his or her own answers.

The faith clarifier is the person who opens up choices for the young person. The clarifier lifts up a moral dilemma, an assumption, a theological issue, or a provocative idea for the young person to consider. And when the young person reaches a decision, that decision is respected, though it may not be one with which the adult agrees.

In clarifying faith, the focus is not upon adults sharing their own faith bias with youth. Clarification requires great sensitivity to the young person's confusion, tension, doubt, or discomfort. It involves helping the young person to identify the problem and to explore alternatives, and then offering resources to the young person as he or she responds.

Being a clarifier requires great trust in God because the adult has little control over the outcome. It requires trust that the nurture of God and of the community of God will revisit the same young person at future times and places that we cannot predict or control. It requires trust that every conversation or interaction with young people need not result in an "answer" or "solution." It requires not expressing every thought you, as an adult, have had on a particular subject. Yet, an adult clarifier is one who offers tremendous empowerment to youth and also one who will likely be respected and accepted as an advocate of faith.

The Clarifier and Advocate as One

Young persons need adult advocates and clarifiers. If youth know that an adult is capable and willing to act in both capacities, they will find ways to let the adult know which they are seeking. The task of the adult is to learn to be sensitive and not to operate on one's own assumptions. Indeed, all persons of faith need advocates and clarifiers.

Parents who have been active nurturers during their children's younger years may likely be viewed by their teenagers as such strong advocates of faith as to not be acceptable as clarifiers of faith. There is nothing necessarily wrong with this, and it simply affirms that youth need a community of faith in which other adults, beyond their parents, are in significant relationship with them.

Young persons are blessed when the same person is both the clarifier and the advocate of faith. If this person has a profound faith commitment but does not force this upon the young person, and if this person encourages thoughtful questioning, then the role of clarifier and advocate will be effectively embodied.

Faith advocacy and faith clarification are important behaviors for those adults who care to nurture adolescents in their faith pilgrimage. Without resourceful adults who are willing to stand in these roles, our efforts in welcoming youth into the faith will lack integrity and effectiveness.

4

Memorable Faith

The church that would establish faith shaping as the most serious ingredient of its ministry with youth must be dedicated to the goal of providing youth the best environment for positive memorable experiences.

MEMORY: your own unique collection of life's experiences
MEMORIES: specific recollections of experiences in your life

One primary way we nurture children and youth is by offering positive memorable experiences. *Faith is brought nearly to young persons by our influence upon their memories.* Memory is a primary difference among children, youth, and adults. An adult has a richer memory from which to draw than a young person or certainly a child. The initial grasp of one's life memories is the beginning of self-identity and a prerequisite before youth can engage in faith shaping. Life's ambiguities arise from reflection upon one's memories.

The Role of Memory

Memory is our own unique collection of life's experiences. Our memory informs our personal identity. The difference between memories, from person to person, is a key reason for our uniqueness as individuals. Memory is the only handle we have to our roots. It is the awareness of our reservoir of memory that is the beginning of the faith journey. As we become aware of what is in that vast reservoir, we attempt to sort it out and to create something meaningful of it.

We will not be able to make mature decisions about ultimate meaning, transcendence, or religious affiliation until we attempt to harmonize our disjointed memories into an understandable memory. A younger child does not yet understand her or his own memory. The child has many disjointed memories that do not connect with one another. For example, a young child will touch a hot oven once or twice. But soon the child remembers (pulls together these separate memories) that a hot oven burns and causes discomfort. Most adolescents are actively involved in the task of making sense of their experience (of understanding their memory). Workers with youth need to help them create order from their experience. Often junior-high-age young persons begin to pull together their faith experiences and memories. They may remember a kindly second grade teacher, a Children's Sunday in the fourth grade, a song they love to sing at Easter, prayers at their family table, and discussions in the sixth grade about the death of a favorite uncle. These separate memories are mulled over in the minds of junior high youth until they are understood. These separate memories are synthesized perhaps into a new belief, or value, or are shaped into a deeper faith.

We cannot be memoryless. We cannot "forget" our lives, though we can certainly forget some of the experiences. We will unconsciously be committing our lives to memory as we go. Not every experience of life is remembered with equal force. Our brains not only have a great capacity for storing memories but also have a selective, or filtering, capability. What we remember from any given experience is largely based upon what we are open to or looking for in that moment. I have no memory at all of my very first date when I was in junior high. Apparently, nothing of any lasting impression happened. I do, however, remember distinctly my first date with my wife because we spent the entire evening in a gas station getting my car fixed! That did leave an impression!

Only the child can control what he or she remembers and its relative significance to him or her. Faith experiences can be forced on youth, but in their memory all that will be retained is the unpleasantness, not the content or meaning of faith.

Early memories influence the way we approach later experiences. A poignant memory of a very bad first date at age thirteen will have some impact upon the fifth date at age fifteen. If we have only memories of dissatisfaction, insensitivity, and carelessness from the first year of life, then we will find it more difficult as teenagers to accept concern, love, and happiness. We are not doomed to live out the past, but neither can we entirely escape it.

As we age and mature, we advance intellectually, relationally, and emotionally. We use these skills to interpret our memories and place them in perspective. The shape of memory is not maturely focused until mid-adulthood. It is shaped by the kinds of experience we remember from our childhood, adolescence, and young adulthood. A memory is shaped by our values, beliefs, and faith.

Faith development must be particularly interested in the memories of youth and children. Consider for a moment the nature of the Christian faith itself. The Bible is a collection of memories and stories told and retold. It is the dialogue of God acting in the history of people.

Without the stories of Adam and Eve, of Abraham moving out, of Moses and the bondage in Egypt, of Jesus' birth, death, and resurrection, . . . of Francis of Assisi, Luther, Bonhoeffer, and King, we would have no faith. Memories of our heritage of faith play such an integral part in Christianity because it is a historical religion. In a similar way personal memories, shaped within each individual, play an integral role in faith development.

If young persons have no important memories of the faith, of the church, of an experience of God, of worship, or of spiritual feelings, they will find themselves in a faith vacuum as young adults.

Influencing the Contexts of Memory and Experience

We can have little impact on how children and youth remember or on what will leave the strongest impression; but we do influence the scope of their experience.

In any civilization it is the responsibility of the adults to provide the contexts for the experience of the children and youth as well as to provide gradual freedom to select their own experience.

Adults cannot dictate all experiences of children or shelter them in any artificial way. Yet in the broadest sense children live within the limits set by the adults around them. Within those limits, in healthy situations, there is granted the freedom for even the youngest of infants to choose and explore. *The prime task of the adult is to set creative limits by determining the contexts for the child's behavior.* Adults should determine that the sandbox is a far better context for a three-year-old to play in than the streets and that social play with other three-year-olds is a better context than sitting passively in front of the television set. The older the child, the broader the limits. Establishing guidelines for dating, for bedtime, for friendships, for homework, and for church involvement all involve a determination of the best context for the child.

For older, mature adolescents, the limits to their experiencing will approach the same limits as those experienced by adults around them: (1) limits of choice and (2) limits set by larger societal conditions. This will occur as adolescents prove themselves capable of handling new responsibility.

From our Christian tradition we want our children and youth to have experienced (1) recognition as a valued and gifted person; (2) love in the active setting of the church and the home; (3) acceptance of themselves as they are; (4) traditions that point toward God and faith; and (5) trust in themselves, in other people, and in God's will. Solid memories related to these five areas should be our goal for all young persons.

The Memories Are for Keeps

The scriptural admonishment is to

> Train up a child in the way he should go,
> and when he is old he will not depart from it.
> —Proverbs 22:6

Not long ago, two very caring Christian parents spoke with me about their son, now a young adult, who expresses no interest in the institutional church or in the Christian faith journey. They were worried that they had done something terribly wrong in his upbringing to cause such disinterest and such denial of his church heritage. They had been parents who tended to influence choices over commitments with their son, but they were superb Christian models. There was no way that their son could have missed their witness. At this point they had not forced the issue with him. I encouraged them to stay in communication and dialogue, never pushing but never dropping their concern. They needed to play a clarifier role. I also tried to help them feel confident in the quality of the memories that this young man carried within him. Someday he will want to sort them out and grow in deeper understanding. If the channels are kept open, the parents could be available to him when the moment of readiness arrives.

As an adult, I am still coming to grips with my own faith memories. For example, when I was in the eighth grade, I worked for Jack, owner of a small store. Jack was a close friend of my family as well as an active church deacon and my Sunday school teacher. One day at the store, Jack was apparently cheated by a wholesale salesman. I remember that he charged into the back room that day raving and ranting in such a way as I had never seen or heard, at least from a Baptist deacon. You might think that this experience convinced me of the hypocrisy or inconsistency of Christian adults, but it had quite the opposite impact.

I was unconscious of this memory until, at the age of twenty-seven, I was writing a sermon. In my preparation I realized what this single memory meant to the shaping of my faith. I learned that day, unconsciously but deeply, that Christians could be real persons. They could get angry in the right place and time. I learned that even my Sunday school teacher could lose his cool and express hostile feelings and still not lose the faith. That recall was a strategic lesson as I was reminded of the important role that memories play in the shaping of faith.

No matter what shape young persons give to their faith and no matter how foreign that might seem to their tutors, young persons will never be able to ignore their roots or memories. They will be a part of those persons wherever they go. Because (1) we can influence the scope of young people's memories and (2) memories are relatively permanent, there are some critically important ramifications for faith development here. All that a church does should be with significance or not done at all! *Boring, mundane experiences are faith defeating!!* What we have always feared is true: a boring offering of the faith will defeat our ability to nurture faith within youth! Not that the criteria is significance, not flash, pomp, or showmanship. If an experience will be significant or profound, the church should consider it.

With children and youth we need intentionally to provide *memorable experiences* (experiences that they will likely remember).

We should be celebrating the Christian seasons in our homes and in our churches with imagination, with tradition, and with significance. We should be creating devotional traditions in our homes and personal lives that really matter! We should plan for some large-scale church events beamed at children and youth. We should live out the faith intergenerationally with potency! We should intentionally encourage strong adult models and create long-lasting relationships between adults and youth in the church, not only between the advisers and youth.

Church school classes that create a life-size replica of the ark of the covenant provide far more potent memories than will those who sit in the classroom describing it for three weeks. Churches that plan a truly personal celebration for adolescents at the time of their baptism will create a lasting impression.

Retreats, camps, trips, conventions, musical or dramatic productions, active mission undertakings, in-depth relationships, significant opportunities for participation in the local church—all are important because of the memorable experiences they make possible.

Expenditures of time and money and talent to create some headline experiences can be defended, particularly for youth. The quality of the memory and the depth of its impact are far more important than the quantity. And this kind of experience does not require a large or sophisticated church. Size and quality are quite unrelated.

The significant experiences need not and should not only be geared to a single age level audience. Personal memories of intergenerational events and relationships are very important. The dedication of a new church building, the participation in a community service project, the washing of Communion cups with one's family each Sunday for months or years—all these can be instructive.

An Inventory of Memorable Experiences

As I think of what I have heard my wife express about the treasured faith memories of her upbringing, I recall these things:

1. the huge youth ministry with a youth-written weekly newspaper that she witnessed as a young child;
2. the annual Palm Sunday service that featured a joyous celebration of and for children;
3. her helping a relative clean up after Communion each month;
4. the faithfulness of her mother in transporting black inner-city children to and from the church;
5. the several adults who took an over-and-above interest in her life;
6. her being employed as an eighteen-year-old Neighborhood Staff member in her church's inner-city recreational program;
7. her own baptism at the same time as her sister's, soon to be followed by her father's baptism;
8. her being in a post-high-school group in which each member was asked to write a one-page statement of faith, which forced her to ask many first-time faith questions; and
9. a youth pastor of her church who faithfully transported her and her sister every weekend for two months to a distant hospital where her father was dying.

Some of her experiences were of the headline variety; some were done with enough repetition to make an impression; some were personally touching incidents, and some were significant relationships.

I would suggest the following as the Inventory of Faith Shaping Experiences which adults should facilitate with youth:

1. *"Headline" Experiences:* highlighted events; occurrences that are noteworthy (they usually require self-discipline and effort from the

youth and concerted planning and support from adults). My wife being employed to do an inner-city ministry by her church was a headline experience for her.

2. *Repetitive Experiences:* those which stand in our tradition; things done with regularity (annually, weekly, daily, seasonally); our ritual. My wife's participation in Palm Sunday celebrations in her church was a repetitive experience. They did the same things and sang the same songs every year.

3. *Personally Touching Events:* feeling-oriented experiences; times when we are deeply affected; times when we are allowed and encouraged to be sensitively in touch. My father-in-law's baptism was a personally touching event for my wife, as was the presentation of her statement of faith to a support group as a young adult.

4. *Significant Relationships:* persons who are of prime importance to us; persons who support and trust us. The youth pastor who transported my wife when her father was dying stimulated a memory of a significant relationship.

Every church, no matter what the size or wealth, can provide a profound inventory of memorable experiences in each of these four categories. Each experience describes patterns of nearness. Some could also apply to directness. (See chapter 3.)

Sometimes we plan specific events that we hope will be memorable for youth, but more precisely we are seeking to create *an environment or atmosphere in which healthy faith shaping can occur.*

Such an environment is not one where adult-youth relationships are merely planned but, rather, one where they are encouraged.

Such an environment is not one where sensitivity is carefully structured but one where persons are encouraged to touch and be touched with their feelings.

In such an environment repetition is not laboriously followed but, rather, is the chosen and desired level of faithfulness.

In such an environment headline experiences are not ends in themselves but are means to a larger goal of faith shaping.

If you could stand in the shoes of your youth for a moment, could you evaluate your church and your family in each area of this inventory?

One difficulty in evaluating progress with adolescents is knowing what will be the long-term impact of these early, shaping experiences. Adolescent faith development is often tentative and unconscious. My wife, for example, resented as a child the intrusion of the inner-city black children

her mother transported. It was only later in her life that this singular witness became a real model and inspiration for her. Effectiveness with
youth (what really makes a positive impact in their lives) is difficult to
evaluate in the short term.

*The church that would establish faith shaping as the most serious ingre-
dient of its ministry with youth must be dedicated to the goal of providing
its youth with the best environment for positive memorable experiences.*

5

Faith Shaping:
How Youth Acquire Faith

Faith shaping is the task of acquiring one's own faith.

AFFILIATING: a child's attempt to identify and stand within the values and faith of the important persons in his or her life

PERSONALIZING: a young person's attempt to claim ownership of his or her own faith in relation to the faith that has surrounded him or her in the formative years

INTEGRATING: an adult's attempt to build the faith she or he has recently personalized upon the faith inherited as a child

FAITH SHAPING: refers particularly to a process during adolescence and young adulthood when most persons actively give shape and substance to their own personal faith; the process of determining one's own faith

FAITH-SHAPING TASKS: a sequence of tasks through which young persons work as they acquire personal faith

EXPERIENCING: encountering spiritual emotions, religious feelings, sacred experiences

CATEGORIZING: sorting out and consolidating one's religious experiences; making sense of the experiences in understandable terms

CHOOSING: deciding what is true and important

CLAIMING: the act of commitment; conversion; giving one's life to something

DEEPENING: the act of maturing in one's faith commitments

SEPARATING: pulling away from earlier convictions and decisions; giving oneself space for reflection and consolidation; rebellion

RESPONDING: gaining a sense of one's life calling; discovering your own giftedness

READINESS: the next level of growth or maturity to which a person is receptive

This chapter focuses upon the heart of this book's concern: the sequence and tasks of growth as youth acquire personal faith. Three postures from which to view the patterns of growth will be considered.

First we will take the posture of a developmental overview of faith. We will sketch the stages of faith as they unfold in the child, the adolescent, and the adult. This posture is the typical developmental one and will undoubtedly parallel those of other contributors [Wayne R. Wood, *On Nurturing Christians* (Nashville: Abingdon Press, 1972); John H. Westerhoff III, *Will Our Children Have Faith?* (New York: A Crossroad Book, imprint of The Seabury Press, Inc., 1976); James Fowler and Sam Keen, *Life Maps: Conversations on the Journey of Faith* (Needham Heights, Mass.: Wexford Press, 1977); John J. Gleason, Jr., *Growing Up to God: Eight Steps in Religious Development* (Nashville: Abingdon Press, 1975); James Fowler, *Stages of Faith* (San Francisco: Harper & Row, Publishers Inc., 1981)]. We will, in the first posture particularly, note those stages leading into adolescence from late childhood and those leading from adolescence into young adulthood.

The second posture focuses upon the adolescent years to describe the specific tasks through which young persons work as they actively give shape and substance to their own personal faith. These tasks form the agenda for adolescents as they pass into this stage of faith maturity. This second posture describes the choices, experiences, decisions, needs, and ambiguities which they face.

The third and final posture will be a glance beneath the stages and tasks of faith development to that which determines growth: individual readiness.

The First Posture: Stages of Faith Development

In this first posture, we will look at the stages of faith development, from childhood through adolescence into young adulthood. A chart at the end of this section will show the relationship of these stages to one another.

Affiliating with Faith

As children mature, most will want to affiliate themselves with the faith tradition that has been practiced and prized in their home and church.

Affiliating is a normal part of childhood. Some persons never wish to affiliate with the church, even when their parents are active in it. There can be a variety of reasons for this. Some of the most common are a feeling of unpleasantness associated with the church, rigid parental attitudes toward religion, or a lax, apathetic attitude toward religious nurture.

Affiliating can be symbolized by the child through confirmation or believer's baptism, or it can simply be a feeling of the child upon which no formal action is taken. It can begin early in childhood or late in adolescence. And affiliating occurs in families whether or not they participate in a church. Parents exhibit faith and values. Children tend to identify with these.

Affiliating is a child's attempt to identify and stand within the values and faith of the important persons in his or her life. There is a developmental tendency within children to affiliate.

Personalizing Faith

At some point, most adolescents will personalize the faith of their parents, creating from this faith something of their own. With many persons, this personalizing begins in middle childhood, becomes more active in adolescence, and peaks in the young adult years. It is prominent throughout the teen years. For most, personalizing is a gradual process. For some it is marked by alienation, hostility, rebellion, and sporadic growth. For others it is calm, reasoned, and cautious. Personality, sexual roles, the surrounding environment, and parental style are the most determinative factors in how personalizing takes place. Two children of the same parents often experience the personalizing of faith in radically different ways.

Personalizing is the young person's attempt to claim ownership of his or her own faith in relation to the faith that has surrounded him or her in the formative years. There is a developmental tendency within adolescence to personalize.

Personalizing is an attempt to claim ownership.

Affiliating is an attempt to claim membership.

As surely as affiliating requires affirmation and acceptance from important others, so does personalizing. With most young persons, personalizing the faith becomes more distinctive the older the young person becomes and the more removed the person is from parental authority. Personalizing requires a self-centeredness, because the adolescent is trying to determine what is uniquely her or his own. This is the reason why adolescents sometimes appear "wrapped up" in themselves.

At the height of the personalizing faith, an older young person might measure her or his growth by how different or opposite it is from the faith traditions she or he affiliated with during childhood years.

Integrating Faith

The surest sign of maturity for young or middle adults is when they measure personal growth *not by how different it is* from the faith inherited from parents, but by *how well their growth builds upon the foundations* laid during childhood years. The pendulum has begun to swing back into a more mature perspective.

Integration is the adult's attempt to build the faith she or he has recently personalized upon the faith inherited as a child. There is a developmental tendency in the adult years to integrate. Integration is the ability to take the good things from one's past and mold them together into a solid foundation for the facing of the future.

The extent of rebellion during the personalizing stage and the degree of difference between one's faith as a child and as a young adult are determiners of the difficulty or ease of the integrating stage. Due to pain or fear, some will postpone this stage until middle-adulthood or beyond.

My own faith pilgrimage can serve as an illustration. I was raised in a small town in the foothills of the Ozark mountains, and the church to which my family belonged included one-third of the town's population. It was a relatively conservative, evangelistic church with strong lay leadership. The pastor came to the church the year that I was born and left when I went away to college. The church had worship services three times a week and revivals three weeks a year. My parents were involved in every phase of the church, and most of our friendships came from the church. Faith was an open discussion in my home, and we maintained daily times of family prayer. As a child, I loved singing the old gospel hymns with gusto. I knew every inch of our church building and enjoyed exploring its many narrow passageways. I was nine years old when I made a profession of faith and was baptized. I knew that my decision deeply touched my father and mother. By the time I was fourteen years old, I had so affiliated with the faith of my heritage that I became a junior advisor to a boys' group at the church.

The dismissal of the popular Sunday church school teacher in the high school department was one of the first things that caused me to distance myself from the faith of my childhood. I became bored with what I felt was the repetitive preaching of the pastor. Worship seemed to be the same old thing. Other youth my age had since dropped out, and even though I continued to participate, I did so critically. When I went to college, I was determined to become involved in as radical an approach to Christianity as possible. It was the 1960s, and opportunities for that abounded. I became a social activist. Among other actions, I picketed the local barber shop for refusing to cut the hair of black students. Whatever was alternative in prayer, music, celebration, or social action, I became involved in it. I had no respect for pastors or the institutional church. These were my personalizing years. I couldn't go home to my childhood church without getting angry. I refused to sing the hymns that I now felt were ridiculous. I was very judgmental of the more conservative leaders of that church. I felt I had outgrown small-town religion.

It wasn't until my late twenties, in sorting through early memories of faith, that I realized that I indeed carried much more of my childhood faith with me than I had heretofore admitted. My first conversation with my pastor during those growing-up years, after a ten-year interval, was shocking. We sat at a dinner party, off to ourselves, two pastors sharing notes. I was stunned to hear him express his ideas of ministry. At first I wondered how he could possibly have stolen my ideas, until I realized that if anyone was the "thief," it was me! Over the next ten years I began a pilgrimage that involved "going back home" emotionally and spiritually. I got in touch again with the best of my memories and traditions from childhood. Now, instead of getting angry when I returned to that church, I became choked with emotion. After an interval of fifteen years, I went back home to preach for the first time. It was likely the earliest opportunity that I could have expressed my profound appreciation for what those people had given me. My faith is still different from theirs, but I appreciate the legacy given me and realize now that I am closer to that tradition than I previously would have admitted. I am well into the integrating stage.

The Broadest Developmental Picture

Let us attempt to stand back for a moment to examine the broadest developmental picture of faith. The chart on the next page shows a typical pattern but is not the only pattern of maturing.

TYPICAL PATTERN OF FAITH DEVELOPMENT

CHILDHOOD YEARS (preschool and primary school years)

- Times of discovering and then affiliating with the values, beliefs, and faith of parents (and church)

LATE CHILDHOOD AND EARLY TEEN YEARS (junior and junior high years)

- Living with the tension of taking the first step beyond a cultural or parental faith bias, accompanied by the most intense desire to affiliate with that bias
- A beginning of self-identify; of will; of asserting one's own person in the initial stages
- Often the young person formally affiliates with faith as "a personal decision" (confirmation/baptism)

MIDTEEN YEARS (high school year)

- An increase in tension between inherited and personalized faith
- Less parental faith influence; more influence accepted from other adults and peers
- Asserting individuality and identity; stepping beyond previous limits
- Often a time to be authentic to one's own chosen faith
- Interest in faith can vary from sporadic to latent to intense during these years

LATE TEEN YEARS AND EARLY TWENTIES (post-high school, college, early career)

- Often attempting to be very untraditional; experimentation with novel ideas of faith; restlessness
- Formulating the most important life directions amidst sporadic and hectic growth
- Rebelling against parental influence and separation from one's own heritage
- Coping with newfound adult independence; recognition of the inadequacy of one's own faith shaping

MIDTWENTIES TO MIDTHIRTIES (marriage, childbearing, establishing vocation)

Years of Most Active Faith Shaping

Affiliation Years

Personalizing Years

Years of Most Active Faith Shaping

Integrating Years

Integrating Years

- Formulating idealistic goals and dreams for life in midtwenties; refining of life goals to more realistic proportions by midthirties
- Integrating inherited faith with personalized faith (Having children and/or becoming a recognized contributor to society often hastens the integration; the question that new parents often ask is, "What is there from my past that I want and do not want my child to experience?")

THIRTIES TO SIXTIES

- Living our the reconciliation between personalized and inherited faith
- Gradual and stable maturation; periods of stagnation and periods of reexamination and change

SENIOR ADULT YEARS

- Broadened understanding and appreciation of life and faith; wisdom ascertained from life's experiences
- Ability to face death and life's consequences with more certainty and less fear
- Ability to gain a larger perspective than one's own personal faith integration

After presenting these stages of faith to different audiences over the years, I maintain that the above pattern reflects the normal stages and typical ages through which most persons pass. But I also recognize that many young women have not been given permission by society to personalize faith in their teens and twenties. Often this is delayed until middle adulthood, creating more anger and confusion. Happily, sexual roles are changing, and young women are increasingly given permission to experience the stages of faith in their more natural sequence.

The Second Posture: Developmental Faith-Shaping Tasks of the Adolescent

"Faith Shaping," as the term is used in this book, does not refer to all phases of faith development, but it refers particularly to those adolescent and young adult years when most persons are actively involved in the task of giving shape and substance to their own personal faith. *Faith shaping is the process of acquiring one's own faith.*

Faith shaping includes a *sequence of tasks* through which young persons pass as they acquire their own faith. These tasks are not unlike the developmental tasks which have been identified by educators:

> A developmental task is a task which arises at or about a certain period in the life of an individual, successful achievement of which leads to his happiness and to success with later tasks, while failure leads to unhappiness in the individual, disapproval by the society, and difficulty with later tasks.[1]

Out of my own pastoral and personal experience I have identified seven tasks which I have seen youth encounter as they shape their faith. I call them *Faith-Shaping Tasks*. These tasks do not describe levels of maturity but, rather, the "work" that one must do to develop personal faith.

The Faith-Shaping Tasks

The seven tasks are in sequence, and most youth will work on the first task before the second and so forth. However, one's passage through the tasks will not occur at an even pace. Some persons will linger longer at one task. Some will delay beginning the faith tasks at all. Some will merge several tasks together while others slide back.

Most adolescents will work forward through these tasks in sequence. However, once they have worked through one task, they will return to that task many more times as they develop and mature in their faith. In truth, these tasks are a continual part of growth, and though faith shaping will lose much of its intensity, many adults work on these tasks throughout their lives. Indeed, if an adult is to keep maturing in the faith, such work is essential. No one ever "completes" the tasks. The only thing final in life's development is death, and Christians don't even feel death is final. We feel that death is only the next step of maturation and development.

Faith-Shaping Task #1: *Experiencing*

Youth years are often filled with intense religious feelings. Spiritual emotions can be sporadic, spontaneous, and superficial. They are also the driving force behind the faith development of youth. Without the wellspring of emotions, faith shaping would lack power. Thus, it is important to recognize that providing a continual reservoir of spiritual experiences is integral to all faith shaping that will occur. A teenager who has had a few religious stirrings is one who has not really entered the faith-shaping process. Religious experiences can happen in worship, at camps, on out-

[1]Robert J. Havighurst, *Developmental Tasks and Education* (New York: David McKay Co., Inc., 1952), p. 2.

ings, while serving others, while singing together, through personal sharing, or at times of quiet retreat.

Nearly all youth have such experiences, though youth who are open to them will obviously have more.

Warm feelings of belonging, of being a part of a family of faith, of appreciation for being loved and accepted and included are all quite frequently associated with this introductory task. The desire to affiliate with the church is often an emotional response. This desire can be nothing more than an introductory religious stirring which needs to be complemented by more serious maturation.

Faith-Shaping Task #2: *Categorizing*

A person enters adolescence with bits and pieces of experiences, of memories, of ideas, and of thoughts. One of the tasks of adolescence is to make some understandable sense of these fragments by pulling them together into more of a whole. This sorting out is often the work of an inquisitive mind. The categories used by youth in early adolescence are frequently simplistic. Their religious thinking might be definite, yet naive. As individuals mature, they return to the task of categorizing. New experiences will cause more sophisticated thinking.

Categorizing is more than an intellectual exercise. Bits and pieces of emotions, attitudes, values, and intentions are also involved in this task. Any effort to consolidate emotions, clarify values, form a coherent memory, or shape an attitude is an effort to categorize experience.

Faith-Shaping Task #3: *Choosing*

Choosing is deciding: "What's important to me?" or "I like this and not that." In choosing is the role of valuing, deciding, and shaping a belief.

Choosing is a natural result of categorizing. After a new idea or experience is comprehended, the teenager chooses it, or believes it. Choosing might have long-term consequences, or it might be quite transitory with adolescents. In faith development, choosing is that time when a young person decides what is true for him or her. Yet the young person has not invested himself or herself in this new idea or truth. He or she is still rather detached from it. For example, in choosing, the young person could decide, "God is good," "Life can be trusted," and "God created the world."

Faith-Shaping Task #4: *Claiming*

In faith development, claiming happens when a young person decides to what or to whom she or he will be true. Claiming is committing one's self to one's choices. Conversion is an act of claiming, of dedicating one's self to follow through on one's choices.

With an adolescent, choosing, categorizing, and experiencing continue, even after faith has been claimed. The youth is still weighing options and valuing. Generally, claiming has a cathartic effect. There is a sense of pride and satisfaction at having arrived at an important milestone. It is often a rich, emotional experience. Sometimes, when young people engage in claiming, they gain a feeling that they "have arrived" and become overconfident.

Faith-Shaping Task #5: *Deepening*

This is the task of growing in the faith—of deepening conviction, commitment, and understanding. Often a teenager will not advance in this area until some time has intervened from the first act of claiming. When some of the newness of commitment has rubbed off and new questions arise, deepening is the task that confronts the person.

The task of deepening is one of working again through the earlier tasks of choosing and claiming, experiencing and categorizing. One is concerned to "update," or replace, naive thinking and commitment. There is a great deal of individuality in the pace of the deepening of one's faith. People grow in unique ways. When deepening occurs in an older adolescent, the overconfidence and "overcertainty" that might have marked the claiming task begin to take on a more mature perspective. Shades of "gray" are seen as opposed to the straight "black and white."

Faith-Shaping Task #6: *Separating*

This task is perhaps most characteristic of older adolescents and young adults. This is the task of setting aside commitments for a time. If an adolescent has worked through the first five tasks, chances are some space will be needed during post-high-school years in which to let one's faith settle. Distance and perspective are now needed. Other alternatives of faith often need to be examined and compared. Rebellion often marks this task. Some youth will swing far away from their roots, as in a pendulum, before resuming a more balanced stance. This distancing is with many young people a necessary task before they can work at synthesizing their rebellion with their roots and enter again the prior faith-shaping tasks.

Rather than being surprised by this separating, rather than labeling it apathy or calling into question the earlier religious activity, one needs to recognize it as a legitimate faith task.

Faith-Shaping Task #7: *Responding*

This is the task of gaining a sense of one's life calling. Here is where one's mission or unique life purpose is considered. What informs this decision is the successful completion of the earlier faith-shaping tasks. For this to be a mature decision, a great deal of deepening and at least some separating have occurred.

At the conclusion of the separating task and the beginning of the responding task, the young person is working hard on developing a new synthesis between the newfound ideas and those ideas traditional to his or her upbringing. The synthesis spurs a new intensity of growth. Sometimes people call this a "second conversion," or a rebirth. It is a renewed commitment at a much deeper level. One feels a need to respond with one's life.

As a responder, these questions are considered: "Where is my calling in life? What have I to give? What can I offer to others and to God? What special role is there for me? Where is my giftedness?"

It is a rare adolescent who enters this task. No adolescent should be pushed into this stage. It is a developmental task far more typical of young adults, though some adolescents will venture into responding.

The "Late Bloomers"

The truth is that some youth will never move beyond the task of experiencing, or even very far into the task of experiencing. They have simply not matured to the point where the shaping of faith is a personal priority. I recall one young boy who was an active participant in my church. His parents were active in all facets of the church. But he simply had not reached the stage of religious experiences, even when he was a senior in high school. He wasn't a slow learner, and he was quite popular with other youth. But he was slow to take responsibility, and he wasn't, at this stage of his life, a very thoughtful or deep person. His situation is not all that rare among youth.

We must accept this. These youth will need to wait until young adulthood before they begin to work on the faith-shaping tasks. And that is all right. For what they develop will probably stand more firmly when done at a more mature age. These "late bloomers" may not have to work through the task of separating.

Adult Responsibilities Relating to Faith-Shaping Tasks

Task #1: *Experiencing* (encountering spiritual feelings)

Try to provide for open-ended expression of feeling.
Encourage feelings that lead to something further.
Allow youth to express themselves openly.
Provide memorable experiences.
Model with your own feelings.
Don't ever let it stop with feelings. As the teenager is ready, encourage
   him or her to move to the next task.

Task #2 *Categorizing* (sorting out feelings, values, experiences, memories)

Do concept studies on Christian ideas. Don't do the work for youth, but
   provide handles.
Be a person who can be trusted.
Never ridicule ideas, no matter how ludicrous they appear.
Be accepting. Don't take everything too seriously.
Be affirming, but do provide honest feedback. You don't need to agree
   dishonestly with everything uttered.

Task #3: *Choosing* (deciding what is true to me)

Encourage youth to think. Challenge them!
Model your own values and choices.
Focus discussions on beliefs that can be prized.
Teach youth how to doubt creatively, and they'll arrive at more authen-
   tic beliefs.

Task #4: *Claiming* (deciding to what I will be true)

Plan many invitations to commitment in a variety of settings.
Talk to youth individually and intimately about their own decisions of
   claiming.
Plan appropriate times of celebration when claiming occurs.
Be certain to provide follow-up support after claiming.
Don't treat claiming as an end in itself but as one step in a lifelong
   process.
Teach youth how to pray and open themselves to transformation.

Task #5: *Deepening* (maturing in the faith)

For youth who are ready, provide appropriate intellectual stimulus.
Don't have high expectations here.
Don't push too soon after conversion. Allow for some "settling in" time.
Share the depth of your faith, your struggles, your questions, your growing edge.
Be a helping and enabling person. Undergird youth with your prayers and support.

Task #6: *Separating* (setting aside faith for a time)

Don't be disappointed or fret unnecessarily as this occurs.
You should express honest reactions, but do give freedom and space to the "separated" youth.
Never let this sever relationships. Open and trusting communication is the great witness. Keep in touch!
Work with parents and others affected by their own sense of guilt, despair, or failure. Help them to see the naturalness of this step.
Celebrate new growth as it occurs.

Task #7: *Responding* (commitment to a life calling)

Encourage this when the person is ready. Initiate only with great sensitivity.
Portray callings as "glimpses" and "visions" rather than facts or certainties.
Study gifts and prayer/meditation with youth.
Always affirm and lift up what you see as a person's gifts, abilities, and talents.
Provide a warm and positive atmosphere for persons to experiment with their own mission and purpose in life.

Adults and the Diversity of the Faith-Shaping Tasks

"How do adults relate with young people at widely varied stages?"
Bill is a senior high church school teacher and a highly regarded one. He is evaluating his last class session with another adult sponsor: "Why is it that this morning's discussion on death and eternal life turned on Susan and Dick and turned off all the others? We had a discipline problem with two of our younger boys, but Susan and Dick just couldn't seem to get enough of it."

The answer could be simple enough: Susan and Dick could be working through the Faith-Shaping Tasks on a different level than the other youth. To Susan and Dick, the "remote" subject of death and eternal life is important because they have already experienced, categorized, chosen, and claimed a faith that deals somewhat maturely with life and daily concerns. Now they are able to venture out into these more distant issues. The other adolescents in the group might include some who have barely begun the faith-shaping tasks, others who would rationalize the entire subject with a naive doctrine, and others who are consumed with more immediate life issues.

What the Faith-Shaping Tasks teach us is to consider youth uniquely. There is no need to become overly concerned that we are not talented enough as adults leaders to attract each person's attention to any given subject. The Faith-Shaping Tasks also teach that we need to have individual and private times with youth. Group times are necessary because youth learn a great deal from socializing with one another. But they also need one-on-one times with adults to work carefully on a personal agenda in a trusting environment.

How do we work with a group of youth at widely varied stages? I would suggest five responses:

1. Think of the diversity as being positive. Because of it, youth can learn from one another. More mature youth are often the best teachers.

2. Don't fret about it. It would be unusual for members of a group to be at the same stage working on the same tasks. Often adults unknowingly use the pressures of group socialization to force a youth group to function at the level of the group's most active and verbal leaders, or at the level in which the adults are most comfortable.

3. Find private times to be with each young person for authentic and deep conversation. Do it regularly.

4. Help the youth to appreciate the diversity and the different concerns each of them brings to the group.

5. Train adults so that they do not expect or strive for uniformity. Adults need to be able to develop an atmosphere where youth are set free to learn from one another and to be able to experience significant dialogue with adult models. Adults need to be trained to recognize the Faith-Shaping Tasks and to help youth as they work through them.

An example might be in order to illustrate these responses. Several years ago, an adolescent named Frank came into our church with his parents. They had not been in church recently, and one of the reasons for his parents' return was because of Frank's problems in their previous community. He had been in trouble with the law, at school, with drugs, and with his parents. Both Frank and his parents saw coming into our community as an opportunity to begin anew.

Frank was a great deal different from the other youth in our group. He had seen a side of life they had never experienced. Frank learned a great deal from the more established youth during his first year. He also had a great deal to offer them from his varied experiences.

In the following years, Frank developed a thoughtful faith. He was balanced, helpful, and insightful. I talked with him personally many times. Finally, I approached Frank about church membership and Christian baptism. He was interested and seemed to understand all the ramifications. He asked solid questions and seemed satisfied with the conclusions he reached.

For some reason in the months that followed he could not make a public decision of faith. As I thought about it, I realized that Frank had worked through the Faith-Shaping Tasks perhaps too smoothly for a person with no church background. I began to wonder if he had sped through his own spiritual development "to be like the other kids." I realized that Frank had a very low level of self-esteem and guilt because of his background in the previous community.

On a retreat one night, Frank and I had occasion to discuss this. I said to him, "Frank, I've been wondering if you think you're worthy enough to call yourself a Christian. Do you think you deserve God's love?" No sooner had I said the words than tears began. A sensitive chord had been touched. In the corner of that lodge, Frank learned about grace. I shared with him my belief that no one deserved God's love. I told him that I had done enough harmful things in my life to keep me forever from the kingdom of love. Only God's undeserved graciousness makes the relationship possible. In dialogue, we both began to understand the hurts of those memories within Frank and how they inhibited him from internalizing what had been so publicly and easily affirmed.

Frank's experience illustrates how diversity among youth and the varied ways youth work through the Faith-Shaping Tasks can be positive. Frank learned a great deal from the group, and the group learned from Frank. At the beginning, we constantly had to help the other youth accept Frank and his uniqueness. Yet it was the private times with Frank that finally penetrated and spurred him to a deeper maturity of faith.

The Third Posture: Readiness, the Way We Grow and Motivate Growth

In this chapter we have explored the stages of faith and the seven Faith-Shaping Tasks which persons must work through in order to shape a mature faith.

What we have not discussed is what spurs human growth. *Our own readiness is what motivates and determines our growth.* We desire stability and balance in our lives. We want things to be in order and in perspective. We want to be able to understand, interpret, and react maturely to all of life's experiences. No person ever fully attains this desired level of balance. Because we cannot and do not, we are constantly bumping up against our own limitations and inadequacies. We must develop a faith in Something that fits the "missing pieces" together. We must depend upon Someone to do for us what we cannot do for ourselves. We recognize we cannot face life's ambiguities alone.

Interestingly enough, it is awareness of our limitations and inadequacies that not only provides our need for faith but also provides for growth. When our lives get out of balance, when we are most restless and dissatisfied, when we enter into a crisis, when we are striving or seeking after something difficult to attain, when we become most aware of our personal potential or an unexplored ability—these are the times when growth is likely to occur.

Developmental scientists call this phenomenon "readiness." Reading readiness has to do with the level of reading a student is ready to grasp. Religious readiness has to do with the level of faith a person is ready to grasp. To ascertain one's readiness is to take one's own "growth temperature."

The dictionary defines "ready" as "prepared for use or for action. Prepared in mind; willing."[1] Our readiness determines to what we are open:
- to what and to whom we will be receptive,
- whether we will address or avoid life's ambiguities,
- in what ways we will be expectant,
- in what directions our hopes and longings will lie,
- and, for Christians, in what direction is God leading.

To be ready for marriage means that I am willing to enter into its commitments. To be ready for college expresses my eagerness to be receptive to what a college has to offer. To be ready to die means that I have come to

[1]Funk and Wagnalls, *Standard College Dictionary* (New York: Funk & Wagnalls Co., 1966).

terms with my own existence and am prepared to meet whatever death holds for me.

Readiness can be seen as a tension, a stirring, a dissatisfaction, a striving, a push from within. Readiness can be determined within a person by developmental limits, intellectual ability, physical ability, emotional maturity, motivation, personal habits, attitude and mood, expectation of others, and spiritual receptivity.

The growth of faith in youth can be traced to their level of readiness: Is the young person ready to be confronted with this moral question? Is she or he ready to make this faith decision? Does this young person want to learn this biblical concept? What is she or he seeking? What troubles him or her?

Human development is really God's timing. God surely is not constricted to our measures of hours, days, minutes, or years. God's "time" is set within us by the tempo of our own development. The stirrings and proddings within us are divinely created and inspired. It is never wrong or sinful to get in touch with one's own readiness. *For to be in touch with the direction of one's growth is to be in touch with God's creative leading.*

The apostle Paul understood readiness, and he wrote of it directly. In his first letter to the Corinthians, he wrote, "As a matter of fact, my brothers, I could not talk to you as I talk to people who have the Spirit; I had to talk to you as though you belonged to this world, as children in the Christian faith. I had to feed you milk, not solid food, because you were not ready for it. And even now you are still not ready for it, because you still live as the people of this world life" (1 Corinthians 3:1-3a, TEV).

The danger we encounter in talking of human development is that we have to generalize and talk about what is typical. Readiness balances that danger by focusing upon what the individual is uniquely and peculiarly ready to encounter.

There are many ways to reflect upon our lives and the growth to which we are most open. The Personal Readiness Wheel that follows describes categories to be used in considering the direction of our growth and of God's leading.

Personal Readiness Wheel

What am I ready for?
   Where are my limits?
   Where is my potential?
What's the next step in my personal growth?

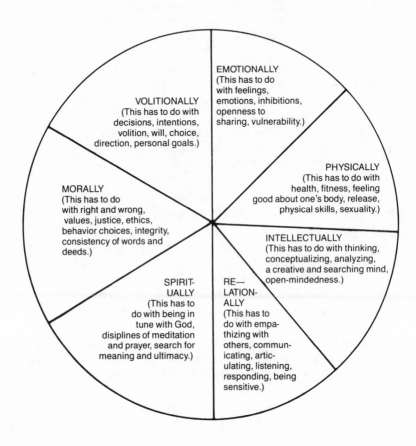

EMOTIONALLY
(This has to do
with feelings,
emotions, inhibitions,
openness to
sharing, vulnerability.)

VOLITIONALLY
(This has to do with
decisions, intentions,
volition, will, choice,
direction, personal goals.)

PHYSICALLY
(This has to do with
health, fitness, feeling
good about one's body, release,
physical skills, sexuality.)

MORALLY
(This has to do
with right and wrong,
values, justice, ethics,
behavior choices, integrity,
consistency of words and
deeds.)

INTELLECTUALLY
(This has to do with thinking,
conceptualizing, analyzing,
a creative and searching mind,
open-mindedness.)

SPIRIT-
UALLY
(This has to
do with being in
tune with God,
disiplines of meditation
and prayer, search for
meaning and ultimacy.)

RE—
LATION-
ALLY
(This has to
do with empa-
thizing with
others, commun-
icating, artic-
ulating, listening,
responding, being
sensitive.)

Our task in youth ministry is to help youth envision faith as a lifelong journey of growth and maturation. This is a difficult assignment because they stand at the very beginning of the journey, and from their vantage, it does not seem like a journey. In far too many churches we unconsciously communicate that faith is a onetime decision completed by baptism or confirmation. Churches of all theological persuasions are guilty.

Since faith and growth both arise as we become more aware of our limitations, faith and growth have a very special relationship to each other. A living faith is one that continually ascertains the next step of growth and attains it. A dead faith is one in which there is no awareness of what one is ready to learn or to experience.

Faith rarely arises out of our feeling adequate about ourselves and in control of our life and world. Faith arises out of our inadequacies, our limits, our finiteness, our seeking something greater than we ourselves are. Faith relates a person or community to the limiting boundaries and to the potential of experience. A truly faithful community is one that lives at its potential. At the outer limits, faith pushes a person to the tension of readiness, to the tension of growth. Dynamic faith for youth or adults is living on the frontierland of our convictions, hopes, and experiences. Moses, Abraham, Ruth, Isaiah, Paul, Mary, and Jesus are all remembered because their faith related them to the limiting boundaries of their lives. They lived "on life's edges."

We must be sensitive to the unique readiness of each young person. Not all we do can be tailor-made for each individual. But neither must we lump all youth together and treat them as identical. The faith needs of one youth will vary greatly from those of another.

How do youth acquire faith? Surely the first appropriate response is that there exists no "one way" to acquire faith. There are as many paths to faith as there are faithful Christians. Who is to say which is best; or who acquired faith in the most mature way? Even though his devout mother attempted to nurture him Augustine spent years in reckless living. However, after he did repent, his life and faith became a beacon to many. We would not advocate that pattern, but we would be foolish to condemn it also.

When a young person is ready to develop faith, let us be there, ready to respond. When a young person needs to be reminded of her or his own potential, or limitations, let us be willing to challenge lovingly, so as to spur personal growth.

Our faith becomes profound when, in the words of Bishop Stephen

Neill of India, we "commit all that we know of ourselves to all that we know of God." That is all that we are ever asked to do.

6

Basics and Beginnings

To nurture children in faith is to help them develop proper handles, tools, and memories so that when they actively engage as adolescents in faith shaping, they will have the needed ingredients to develop a mature faith.

THE BASICS APPROACH: an attempt by adults to present a "simplified adult faith" to children

THE BEGINNINGS APPROACH: an attempt by adults to present an appropriate grounding and foundation for children, to be used in future faith development

We cannot understand what must happen in faith development with youth until we comprehend what must happen in this area with children. One age truly is the foundational stone for the other. What we try to accomplish in faith development with youth is built directly upon what we accomplish with children.

There is and must be a substantive difference between the faith nurturing of children and that of youth. The childhood years are the storing, collecting, incubating years. Adolescents use those foundations to internalize, personalize, or shape their faith.

The Two Approaches with Children

The most effective method of faith development with children is a foundational method I call the *Beginnings Approach*. The beginnings style emphasizes bringing faith nearly to children, rather than directly, until they are developmentally ready to respond to the directness.

The more familiar approach, however, I call the *Basics Approach*. Many adults, so influenced by the desire to evangelize children, believe that the most effective approach is a full presentation of the gospel as early as possible. They reason that the younger one is who claims the faith, the better. They believe we should bring children both "nearly" and "directly" to the story of faith.

The *Basics Approach* is characterized by these assumptions:

1. Children need to be presented with the gospel as completely and as early as possible. They need to be taught the simple basics and fundamentals of adult belief and doctrine.

2. Children have a need for a personal faith. They are capable of accepting or rejecting the gospel. They are ready to enter into the Faith-Shaping Tasks of Claiming and Choosing.

3. The best way for children to learn about faith is for it to be told to them directly, clearly, and unashamedly.

4. The best way to respond to children's questions and strivings is to answer them once and for all.

5. The emphasis in childhood is upon constructing a faith.

These assumptions sound reasonable and helpful. It is upon these assumptions that much of our faith development with children is now based.

The *Beginnings Approach* has another, quite different, set of assumptions:

1. The emphasis in childhood is upon preparing for faith. It is a time to prepare a repertoire of memories rich in faith potential. It is a time to bring faith and its traditions near to children.

2. Children do not yet have a need for adult faith. They have not yet experienced real uncertainties or limitations about themselves. They do not have a firm grasp of their heritage, experiences, or memories. Adolescence is normally the earliest age at which they enter into intentional faith shaping, taking responsibility for their lives.

3. Children will sometimes want to covenant with their church in a desire for affiliation and belonging, but making lifelong commitments is normally an adolescent or adult task.

4. Children need to be presented with beginnings to faith: isolated handles, tantalizers, feelings, concepts, tools, and memories to be used at a later age to form a personal faith. Complete formulations are confusing to children. They tend to think with more immediacy, in bits and pieces. They do not have the connecting, summarizing, or theologizing ability of adults.

5. Faith is not a set dogma or creed to be accepted or rejected. It is something that needs to be personalized by each believer; ". . . religion is

not something grafted superficially onto the personality; religion is what the whole person becomes by its growth. . . ."[1]

6. Formal learning needs to be responsive to the readiness of the individual. Providing answers to questions that have not and are not being asked can be smothering to future growth.

Comparing the Two Approaches

When we look at our children, we see they are unspoiled, innocent, and easily influenced. Children seem eager to please and to be obedient to adult will. Faith commitments "appear" to be much easier for children than for adolescents. This is because the teenagers have so many more things to consider when they enter into a faith commitment. *We must be careful to provide children with what they need rather than what we want.*

In our faith we should not be apologetic: We would like for our daughters and sons to accept faith in our Lord Jesus Christ. We would like for them to accept our faith bias.

And so, what do we do? Shall we present our children with the gospel so true, simple, and constant down through centuries? Shall we present the basics of the gospel directly to children? What else can we do?

Presenting children directly with the "simple and complete gospel" is not only inadequate but also inappropriate if we are hoping for them seriously to accept the gospel later in life when they are more able to do so.

Too often we have wanted to convert children on our time schedules instead of allowing God to do the converting on God's natural developmental "time schedule." We structure Christian education for children as if they are "little adults" because we are afraid they will miss what we have to tell them. We do so because of our lack of faith in God. We are unwilling to give to God what is important to us: our children. Yet our children are not created in our image but in God's image. God is the only keeper of the clock of readiness. Persons are ready for different challenges at each stage of life. Everything has a season (see Ecclesiastes 3).

If I were to teach an adult who has never heard of Christianity, I would tell him the very basics of my faith—what it means to me and what it can mean to him. I would use the simplest and most basic words. I would teach him Christian symbols and their meanings. But an adult has capabilities that children do not.

To nurture children in faith is to help them develop proper handles,

[1]R. S. Lee, *Your Growing Child and Religion* (New York: Macmillan Publishing Company, 1963), pp. 136-137.

tools, and memories so that when they actively engage as adolescents in faith shaping, they will have the needed ingredients to develop a mature faith. This is the Beginnings Approach because it stresses that a personalized faith can have its beginnings in the childhood years but will be given substance only as the child moves into and beyond adolescence.

What can happen to children educated by the Basics Approach?

1. They will probably get answers before they have questions, and thus when they do naturally ask their own questions of faith, the answers they have received will sound trite.

2. They might conclude that Christianity is complicated and unreal, that faith is unrelated to the real concerns of life.

3. Since they will find it nearly impossible to be true to a faith commitment at their age, they might learn an artificial separation between belief and behavior.

4. Later in life some will feel that they have been exploited and manipulated in having been encouraged to join the church and profess faith. The decision they made will now lack meaning, and thus faith will lack meaning.

5. They will have received Basics at such an early and superficial age that some will never be able to extend their faith to a deeper level, even in their adult years. It will be frozen and hollow.

What can happen to children nurtured by the Beginnings Approach?

1. Their curiosity will be whetted. They can arrive at adolescence with questions that have not yet been answered!

2. They can learn earlier that faith must be personalized and internalized. No one else can do it for them.

3. As adolescents, they will likely be ready emotionally, volitionally, and developmentally to engage in faith shaping. They will have been given the proper skills and tools to engage in the task.

4. They may be willing as children to make a covenant with their church to be "beginners in faith."

5. They can discover the church and Christianity to be rich in human experience—natural, and a part of their real world.

If we conclude that the Beginnings Approach is most appropriate, what happens to the Basics? We cannot and should not dismiss the Basics. The youngest children need to see adult faith in action. They need to hear it preached, see it demonstrated, and modeled as a possible goal for themselves. *They need to be near Basics but not have the approach aimed directly at them.*

The Shape of the Beginnings Approach

Let's explore the specifics about what Beginnings in faith development can mean. What will it look like in church education?

It will be focused on developing these handles, experiences, and tools that children can use as they mature:

1. *Bible Stories.* In the Beginnings Approach we are not striving for a holistic understanding of the Bible. We do, however, want children to be very familiar and comfortable with the Bible. We should emphasize those parts that they can easily understand: parables, stories, and incidents rather than highly symbolic passages (e.g., emphasize Paul's travels, actions, and personality rather than his theological formulations). The Bible will become a loved book full of exciting incidents, real people, and an exciting and real God. It will not seem distant, hard to read, or complicated. In the Beginnings Approach, the child's interpretations will be accepted and nurtured.

2. *Adult Faith as a Model.* Children can observe the faith of adults in worship, in congregational life, in mission, and use it as a model for their own faith development.

3. *Concept Education.* Children need to develop key Christian concepts which are a basic part of the foundation for a future faith. It is essential to refine such concepts as life, love, sharing, caring, death, right and wrong, hope, honesty, joy, peace, anger, pride, power, wonder, God, the Bible, church, and promise. Their curriculum could help them explore a concept by reading about it, acting it out, playing games based upon it, "crafting" things from it, relating it to life, and testing it upon life.

4. *The Child's Natural Ability to Wonder, to Question, to Create, to Imagine, and to Initiate.* Helping children be creative, imaginative, and curious will give them specific skills to use in faith shaping as adolescence approaches.

5. *A Rehearsal at Interpreting Life's Experiences.* Children are very curious. They often ask "Why?" "How?" and "When?" Practice at interpretation of experiences is the beginning of of a faith-shaping skill. Encourage their interpretation skills.

6. *A Rich Repertoire of Memories.* Use the same variety of memories as suggested for youth in chapter 4: headline experiences, repetition experiences, personally touching events, and significant relationships. The patterns of nearness are similar for children and youth.

7. *A Warm, Inviting, Welcoming Family of Faith.* Such a church family affirms children where they are and with integrity launches them on a lifelong journey as persons of faith.

Summary

Emphasis on basic doctrinal interpretations can be counterproductive because the memory is formed by the child and not us. All the child might remember is the unpleasantness with which we forced the issue.

Many post-high-school youth who have grown up in the church have unpleasant impressions. Many of those who have experienced the Basics Approach feel faith to be manipulative, adult dominated, irrelevant, and stilted.

Beginnings to faith can be offered to children in the context of an adult community of faith. They will see and hear the Basics from that adult community, but they will not be expected to embrace all that basic faith represents for adults.

There are some churches that are guilty of never allowing children to see or witness the Basics of adult faith. These are the churches that separate the children from the adult community when it worships, studies, and fellowships. There are homes where children are taught to pray the familiar childhood prayers but never hear authentic prayers from their parents.

Children need to experience an *introduction to faith* (Beginnings) while at the same time experience the *destination of their faith journey: adult faith* (Basics). It is no better to clobber children with exclusive Basics than to "underwhelm" them with exclusive Beginnings.

Good church school curriculum emphasizes Basics for the first time in the junior high years. This is the appropriate time for the faith to be presented directly. What a joy it is to be able to present the story of Christian faith when adolescents have spent their childhood years in preparation for it! What a joy not to find the terrain cluttered with earlier attempts to push religious commitment ahead of God's natural timing!

Beginnings are a tool of nearness and should be emphasized during the childhood years as the foundation upon which the Basics of faith can be presented—fresh, alive, and new, when adolescents are most able to embrace faith.

7

Giftedness: A Unique Faith-Shaping Agenda

Teenagers should be developing their minds, talents, bodies, and feelings. They should be developing their capacity to relate, to create, to search, to give thanks. With the proper mind-set, these are all acts of a developing faith.

GIFTEDNESS: all of the personal resources with which God has endowed you

The Faith-Shaping Task of Responding (discovering one's life calling) has its roots in giftedness. In chapter 5, the task of Responding was described as primarily a young adult task. Yet this important Faith-Shaping Task is motivated and enriched by an emphasis in the teen years upon giftedness.

Giftedness is all the ways that God has invested divine nature in each human life. Faith in God and giftedness are partner convictions. If we enter into a relationship with the God of love, then the next step of faith is to believe that God has endowed us with many resources for the living of our lives. God created us and endowed us! All personal resources which we enjoy and use are thus seen as gifts from God.

When Youth Understand Their Giftedness

Youth enhance their faith reservoir by developing their God-given giftedness. *If youth understand their talents, resources, and abilities as gifts* (not "I am talented" but "I am gifted"), *then the unfolding of God's gift is a matter of faith development.*

Faith involves more than a private, spiritual endeavor. Faith involves the unfolding of the totality of one's life and being. *Christian faith is coming to know* (1) *how God has invested in us* and (2) *how we can invest*

75

ourselves in God's way. Faith ultimately requires responding to the direction of God's leading.

The teen years are a prime time, perhaps *the* prime time of life, to begin to see one's personal resources as gifts and to explore the meaning of those gifts.

Our personal resources are primarily interior, i.e., what is within us. However, our resources also include what's exterior: body, possessions, environment, etc. For the teen, standing at the edge of adult life, most of the resources will be one's own person (not belongings, status, or possessions)—body, mind, personality, talents, skills, interests, volitions, creativity, initiative, inclinations, dreams, expectations, behavior, self-discipline, and feelings.

The development of these personal resources *can be* a faith-shaping task. The popular or humanistic understanding of these resources would be to view them as "happenstance" or as "something one has deserved or earned," or as "something innately human," or as "that which makes one unique," or as "that which one has inherited or acquired." Some of these observations might be partly accurate.

But Christians, on the other hand, view these resources as gifts. Christians see them as undeserved gifts from a loving God who has freely *endowed* human life with *potential.* God gives the raw materials of personality and ability; God gives the undeveloped capacity to feel, to develop physically, to uncover talents.

If we view our personal resources as unearned gifts, if we understand that a loving God has given them to us with the divine intention that they be developed and used for the right purposes, then we are likely to feel both grateful and energized.

We will not feel cocky or conceited with all the resources we were smart enough to acquire. We acknowledge that they are gifts to us.

We will not feel cheated when we see someone else excel where we do not because we realize that individuality of giftedness. We excel in ways they do not.

We will not feel selfish as we realize that what we have is not to be used only for our own desires, lusts, or ambitions.

We will not feel alone, thinking no one truly knows our potential or understands how it can be used.

If young persons begin to understand their giftedness, they are learning God's plan for their lives; they are beginning a lifetime of thankfulness for all that has been so freely given to them.

Teenagers should be developing their minds, talents, bodies, and feelings. They should be developing their capacity to relate, to create, to search, to give thanks. With the proper mind-set these are all acts of a developing faith.

Nothing is more exciting than to see a teenager sing her first solo and with pride realize, "I'm good!"—Nothing more exciting than to watch a young girl practice for hours and months and finally make the school basketball team!—Nothing more exciting than to see a son bring home his first painting from art class!—Nothing more exciting than to see a new bit of wisdom arise from the ashes of a first broken relationship. God must surely smile at those times, watching the development of divine creation!

The development of one's gifts is one of the most important tasks of adolescence. If we discourage teenagers and thwart their potential they will carry scars for the rest of their days. Consider how much time young persons spend each and every day developing their gifts! One young girl I know, while perhaps not typical, attends modern dance rehearsal after school four times a week. She now teaches younger ones to dance. She plays the clarinet and rehearses and performs at that extensively. She is taking advance-level weekly piano lessons. She's holding down her first job, developing abilities as a responsible employee. She attends high school full-time, developing intellectual abilities. She dates and participates actively in the church fellowship group, pruning and shaping her relational skills. She interacts frequently with adults in the church community, thereby learning that ability. She sings in the church choir and participates in the bell choir with other youth. Many youth spend extraordinary amounts of time and energy developing their giftedness. It perhaps is one of the most common traits of adolescence.

Gospel Logic About Giftedness

I have always felt that we place the emphasis in the wrong place in the story of Jesus' feeding the five thousand by the shores of the Sea of Galilee. We look at the little lad with five loaves and two fishes, at his willingness, and we look at the miracle, Jesus expanding the food.

The point of the story often missed is to be found by looking at the disciples. The incident happened early-on in the disciples' ministry, according to the account in Mark's Gospel. Jesus had sent the disciples out for the first time, two by two, to minister and preach in nearby towns. It is obvious they were inexperienced by the elemental instructions Jesus gave them. The subsequent beheading of John the Baptist must have left them feeling insecure and fearful.

When they returned from the ministry in nearby towns and villages, they were weary and tired. So they climbed into a boat, and Jesus took them to a remote area to get away and relax. But the crowds raced on ahead of them; so anxious were they to see Jesus! And Jesus had such compassion on the waiting crowd that he set aside the weariness of the disciples for the needs of the people. A long day went by, full of crowds pushing and pressing against Jesus and his tired disciples. On such days the disciples probably did little more than attempt to manage the crowds, assist Jesus, and troubleshoot all the inevitable problems.

As the day wore on, the disciples came to Jesus, worried, and said, "This is a lonely place. These people need food. Send them away." And Jesus said, "Give them something to eat" (Jesus obviously knew the disciples had no physical food at their disposal.) And the disciples replied sarcastically, "Do you want us to spend a life's savings to feed these people dinner?" But Jesus was concerned with more than food.

So he asked them, "How much do you have? Go and see." And the disciples went out and looked only for that which satisfies physical hunger. They looked for material food. And they brought back five loaves and two fishes from a small lad. Even amidst their searching, these were all the resources that they could find. Jesus sighed. "Get these people seated." And he looked up to heaven and asked a blessing, "Father, bless the food that satisfies soul and body." And he broke the bread, and in the breaking of the bread and the distributing of the fish, the food expanded to fill the need.

Scripture says, "[The disciples] were completely dumbfounded, for they had not understood the incident of the loaves. Their minds were closed" (Mark 6:52, NEB).

Jesus sensed the people's spiritual needs, and he sensed the people's physical needs, and he could not and did not separate the two. And he saw that it was his mission to meet the needs of the body and soul and to ask of those who were his disciples, "In the midst of the needs of this world, how much do you have?"

Jesus was attempting to teach his own disciples in this incident. First, he had challenged them to go out, two by two, with no other resources than that of their own faith and their own abilities. Then, he challenged them to respond on faith to the needs of the crowd. He wanted them to see beyond the puniness of the five loaves and two fishes to the majesty and wonder of food to feed body and soul.

Jesus was attempting to be responsive to the giftedness of that moment; the disciples couldn't see beyond the frenzy of the moment.

Jesus was asking the disciples, "How has God gifted you for this moment? What resources has God laid at your disposal?" Most of us see our resources as *our* possessions, *our* talents, *our* skills. And so do youth. Jesus was asking his disciples to look at the very same resources and see them as gifts.

Giftedness is the point of this story! Giftedness is how much God has invested in our lives. We were set forth on our earthly trek with the giftedness to be able to meet the demands of each day. And in this context, it is a sin not to recognize our gifts, or to develop our gifts, or to volunteer our gifts.

There was a difference between Jesus and his disciples on that remote hillside in the middle of a huge crowd. It was the difference between a frenzied, frantic, and worried group attempting to respond to the problems of the moment and a concerned, loving, receptive, prayerful person who on faith responded to those about him.

There's some "gospel logic" about giftedness that can be drawn from this story that has tremendous implications for youth, who, like the disciples, are young in their Christian experience. Jesus could just as well be teaching these five points about giftedness to youth today as he did to his disciples. (The word "have" is used here not to refer to the possessions but to the totality of what God has given to a person.)

1. *We have more than we think we do.*

The first premise of giftedness is that we are not in touch with all the potential that God has given to us. Indeed, when we feel insecure or unworthy, we are often not aware of all the value, the esteem, and the giftedness God created in us. "He who sows sparingly will also reap sparingly, and he who sows bountifully will also reap bountifully" (2 Corinthians 9:6). The disciples were stuck because they could find only the obvious—five loaves and two fishes.

One of the most common traits of adolescents is insecurity about themselves: "Am I OK? Am I acceptable? Am I worthy?" These are critical life issues for youth. Jesus is telling them: "Your giftedness is far greater than you think it is." Youth are just beginning to uncover all of their talents and abilities. They are often at tenuous stages of development, reminded more of their limitations than their capabilities.

2. *The more we give, the more we have.*

That doesn't make any sense at all, and it never has. Jesus said in Luke 6:38: "Give, and it will be given to you." In the youth musical "How Free Is Free?" the Fool, the main character, says these lines to the cast: "Oh . . . . and don't forget to continue to look to your Father so that you can receive and understand more of Him, so that you can give more. . . . the more you receive [your giftedness], the more you have to give, and the more you give, the more you can receive."[1] This is the main point in the story of the feeding of the five thousand. The more we give, the more we have. The more open we are to God's giftedness, the more we have to share with others. Youth discover their purpose in life as they give of themselves to others.

3. *We've got to know what we have in order to give what we have.*

Jesus told the disciples, "Go and see how much you have." The disciples thought all they had was five loaves and two fishes. They didn't realize all the other resources available to them. How tiny youth think their own resources to be! Christians must be people continually becoming aware of their own giftedness: their own ability to share and give their talents and abilities. Youth need to be aware that when they are not growing in self-awareness and discovery, then they are not going in God's way.

4. *Our own gifts need to be called forth by others. They will recognize our gifts before we do.*

We must be people who call forth the gifts of one another—youth to youth, adult to youth, youth to adult. We must be intimate and honest enough with one another so that we can recognize a new ability bursting forth or see a promising new direction for service. Most of us are ignorant and blind to our own giftedness until someone else points us toward it. Whenever we call forth the gifts in others, we are allowing God to work through us. Youth are normally willing and open to allow others to call forth their gifts. We need only find more sensitive adults available to do it.

5. *The only way to use effectively what we have is to volunteer what we have.*

Matthew 10:8 (KJV) says, "Freely ye have received, freely give." There are times when people need to be asked to do something because we are attempting to call forth their gifts. Jesus asked the disciples to go out two by two because he thought they would discover something exciting about their own ministries and abilities. But the more normative pattern in a church should be that people come forward to say, "I want to be used. I want to help." We're always so worried that people will think we're too conceited or pushy when we volunteer ourselves. Or we're frightened that if we volunteer to do one thing, the church will ask us to do everything else. Too many people are caught up with the question "What are *they* going to ask me to do?" rather than "How can I be of service?

[1]"How Free Is Free?" a youth musical. Lyrics and script by Errol Strider, music by Michael Brandt. Property of Creative Spirit, Inc., 1520 Euclid Avenue, Boulder, Colorado 80302.

How can I put to work the resources God has given me?" Our words to youth will not do much good, but our actions will. Strong adult modeling will effectively communicate the right way for them.

When Jesus asked his disciples, "How much do you have?" he meant in that question all of these things. He meant to tell them, "You've got more than you think you do. If you'll give more, you'll receive more. You've got to 'go and see' what you have in order to give what you have. If you'll trust me, I can call forth your giftedness. I can see it more clearly from my vantage point than you can from yours. And, finally, don't send the people to someone else to be fed; feed them yourselves. Volunteer what you have to meet the physical and spiritual needs of people."

Contexts for Faith Nurturing

An intentional bias is one which we shape that provides the most whole-some environment for the nurturing of faith.

Every setting of our lives has its own inherent bias. The homes, the school, the community, and the working environment are spaces filled with particular biases. No environment or context is neutral.

Persons concerned about nurturing faith with youth can shape an "intentional bias" in at least several important contexts of their lives. The bias should be that which is most facilitative as young persons shape their own personal faith.

A good schoolteacher creates an intentional classroom bias. Such intentionality is reflected when a teacher says, "In my classroom it is always appropriate to ask tough, probing questions." When Scripture says, "As for me and my house, we will serve the Lord," it, too, reflects an intentional bias in the family or clan. If a coach says to her players, "Winning is important because it motivates us to play our best. But our real purpose is to play hard, play fair, and play to learn, whether winning or losing," that reflects her intentional bias. If a family decides to make each Friday evening a family recreational night and resolves that a time of praying, sharing, and Bible reading will occur three evenings each week around the dinner table, that also provides an intentional bias.

A New World for Youth

Youth today live in a new world in many ways. The settings in which the average teenager lives his or her life are often so conflicting and confusing that they leave many youth drifting in search of roots. No longer can we assume harmony even between the church and the home, or the home and the school, or the church and the youth peer culture. A new approach to nurture is needed in this area.

We need to expose youth to *loving families* where faithfulness is a natural part of daily living and where faithful traditions are maintained. We need to expose youth to a *loving church family* where they are accepted as full participants, where their contributions are valued, and where the stories of faith are told in ways that are accessible to young people. We need to expose youth to the *world family of God,* where each person, regardless of culture, color, income, sex, or geography is valued and where each nationality, society, denomination, and race is accepted for the unique contribution it makes to the body of Christ in the world.

The settings that best offer themselves as contexts for intentional faith nurture may vary from situation to situation. Generally, we can create an intentional bias for nurture of youth in the home, in the church, with the youth peer group, and as part of the global family of Christ.

Faith Nurturing in the Home

The home includes one's primary family. Its influence is pervasive on most young people. All parents, consciously or unconsciously, establish a bias in their home that affects all areas of the young person's development. When parents are conscious and intentional about this bias, they can be more assured of the nurture they provide. Parents need to decide about the faith traditions that will be practiced in the home. New parents should receive guidance and training from more experienced parents in how to do this. Often this can happen as adults return to the church themselves at the occasion of the birth of their first child. Frequently, this means a renewed spiritual commitment for themselves as well as the nurture of their first child.

Homes can be places for traditions of nearness and the practice of directness. All four types of Faith-Shaping Memories can be provided in the home: headline experiences, repetitive experiences, personally touching events, and significant relationships.

Faith can be uplifted and celebrated in the home. Worshipful and joyful celebrations of new births, baptisms, decisions of faith, transformations, graduations, beginnings, and endings can occur in the home. Gratitude for the gift of daily life can be authentically expressed.

A home should be a place where Christian friends and a Christian support community gather. All of this should not occur only at a church building. Pastors and other important persons of faith should be seen in the home. Symbols of faith can be prominently displayed. Sharing times, family nights, daily devotions, meal prayers, late-night discussions, and families attending church together all can create this intentional bias.

One of the most classic problems is found in situations in which the parents were brought up in strict moral and spiritual environments in their childhood years and eventually outgrew this perspective. Now they raise their children in reaction against this upbringing. The consequence is that the children are raised uninformed as to the parents' actual faith commitments. The practices of nearness are absent. There are many parents who so value freedom of choice for their children that the children grow up without any exposure to the parents' deep reservoir of faith.

Parents, at a minimum, need annually to tell the story of their faith to their children and youth at the level of each young person's maturity.

Many parents become so involved attempting to offer their children every opportunity to develop athletic, artistic, or scholastic gifts that the development of faith is pushed to a minimal priority. Regardless of how wholesome other activities may be, if we concentrate on building the frame and structure but ignore the foundation, the building will eventually crumble. We will produce talented and well-educated young people who have no sense of their own roots, no inheritance of faith from which to draw as they face the challenges of adolescence and adulthood.

Faith Nurturing in the Church

Many churches today have a blurred sense of their own identity and mission. Not knowing how to deal creatively with diversity and individuality, they attempt to be all things to all people. Their sense of corporate mission lacks focus and substance, with the agenda being set by forces beyond the congregations themselves. The maintenance and management of a church's institutional life burdens many congregations as a first priority. Churches that are experiencing renewed life and hope are doing so as they articulate their reasons for being and the special focus of God's call for their congregations. As a church gains a clear sense of its mission, the children and youth within it will have a deeper understanding of the intentional bias of that community of faith. They will experience the church as a people of mission and will find themselves involved in that mission as well. The adults will be much better able to model for their young people the values and commitments of that community of faith.

As we consider youth involvement in the church, we must recognize that most young people do not participate by their own free choice. For most youth, someone else selected that church for them. When a family does relocate or change churches, young people should have a voice in that decision (though it is also important for them to hear and understand their parents' needs related to church affiliation). The parents' influence over the selection of a congregation and the style of the family's participation (which was decided long before the child was old enough to have a voice) is critical in empowering the intentional bias that the church offers to that young person. A parent who cares deeply about the community of faith will naturally open more doors and offer more handles for his or her children to follow in faithful participation. *The church's ability to offer an intentional bias of faith is significantly influenced by the commitments and choices of the parents.*

The church family should be a special community of grace where youth feel accepted, prized, and included. It should be a place for friendships of all ages. It should be a place where intergenerational relationships grow and mature. It should be a context in which a number of adults, including those with no special leadership responsibilities with youth, take seriously their relationships with young people. A congregation does a great disservice when it completely delegates nurture of children and youth to specialized age-level ministries. Youth rarely witness examples of faith except those of their peers and adult volunteers. *Youth can never find their place within the traditions and stories and values of the community of faith when they are kept on its periphery.*

Parents and leaders should expect involvement from youth in the church. For younger youth, the adult role is more definite and authoritative. For older youth, accountability must never be abandoned, though more choices and personal space must be introduced. Youth need to know how much their parents and leaders care that they are involved in the community of faith and how much it means to the adults precisely because of the unique contribution that young persons make. For older adolescents and young adults who are in the Separating task of faith shaping, freedom must be granted regarding their faith commitments and participation. However, these youth still need to know that parents and leaders care and that they value faith in Christ with ultimate significance, even as in love and trust these young persons are given the space to make their own decisions.

Faith Nurturing with Adolescent Peers in the Church

The peer group is perhaps where churches have traditionally focused most of their attention and developed the best nurturing resources and practices. It is a significant context for developing patterns of nearness and directness. Adult faith clarifiers are often youth group sponsors.

The adolescent peer group in the church is a pivotal setting for providing faith-shaping memories. Many church-sponsored youth groups plan headline experiences for youth, such as mission trips, youth musicals, camps, or retreats. They provide repetitive experiences through group traditions and practices passed along throughout the years of junior and senior high. They are a context for personally touching events and, of course, significant relationships with both peers and adults.

One important factor in creating an intentional bias for the adolescent peer group in the church is the adult sponsor. These dedicated persons can be very influential models and deserve the support of the entire congregation for this unique calling. They will often be advocates and clarifiers of faith with young people. They will guide youth as they work their way through one faith-shaping task after another. They will assist a young person who is receiving God's call and walk with him or her through the process of transformation. *The adult sponsor is one of the first and few adults who aren't in a position of hierarchy over the youth with whom most young persons can form a deep friendship.* Adult workers with youth and young adults should be trained in developing relationships in which authority, accountability, and mutuality are shared with youth. What makes the adolescent peer group in the church unique is the possibility of a context that is free of a hierarchy of authority over the youth. Obviously this becomes more possible with older youth than with younger youth.

A church peer group is often a collection of adolescents who do not see one another except at church and who might not share common interests nor run "in the same crowd." They may not have chosen to be friends if it were not for the church relationship. When this relationship occurs, it is one of the rare settings where teenagers relate to their peers on the basis of pluralism. Due to the lack of self-esteem, most youth will not choose such pluralism among their friendships at school because it is too threatening. The diverse personalities and interests make the church adolescent peer group an exceptional opportunity for tolerance, patience, growth, and understanding.

Peer ministries in the church should be fun, active, recreational, and missional. Youth also need to be focussed upon personal sharing, worship, prayer, and reflection. The balance should be maintained. Adults should be neither embarrassed nor manipulative about introducing the agenda of faith.

Adolescent peer groups in the church can exert a significant influence in the lives of young people far out of proportion to the amount of time spent with the group. These peer ministries are one of the few places where faith intersects with the popular youth culture that young persons experience in other contexts.

Faith Nurturing with a Global Perspective

The church is one of the few global organizations to which youth can belong. Not only is the church global in the sense that there are members of it in nearly every culture and continent, but we believe that Christ is present and active throughout the world. Christ is the Lord of life and Savior of the world. Because of our Western orientation, which prizes the worth of each individual, we have tended to re-interpret the gospel as if it were concerned only with individuals. Youth need to understand that God loves the world and sent Jesus into the world for the sake of the world. Ours is a cosmic God with a global message of love and reconciliation.

More and more, youth will belong to an intercultural church. We are rapidly growing beyond the traditional ideas of mission-sending and mission-receiving churches. Already, Third-World Christians are speaking to Christians in the First World. Certainly the church of the twenty-first century will be a global church in every sense of the imagination. It will be difficult to be a member of a neighborhood church and be unaware of the global nature of the gospel and of the church of Jesus Christ.

In enlightened churches today youth can gain a unique world view that may be unavailable to them through any other context. These churches will be empowering youth to build bridges and connections to young persons in other cultures, whether across the city or across the world. These youth can understand the world in more accepting and connectional ways than a school geography class could ever offer. They can understand that a young person in Zaire or Manila can stand in relation to the very same God, expressing their faith in utterly distinct ways. They can feel "at one" with God's people everywhere. Young persons in these churches can know that they are citizens of the world and citizens of God's commonwealth in the world.

Culture Shaping

We will not do justice to adolescents unless we help them consider the shape of their emerging faith in relation to their culture.

CULTURE: values and assumptions that we share with others that enable us to live in community

We have explored faith shaping as an individual concern. We have previously stated that faith shaping refers "to those adolescent and young adult years when most persons are actively involved in the task of giving shape and substance to their own personal faith." We have recognized that this need not be a private undertaking. We will have failed young people if their faith shaping has only been done privately. Faith shaping can be consciously nurtured within one's faith community.

We are more than solitary individuals, and certainly this is true of adolescents who usually define themselves in relation to other people and the expectations of others. More specifically, we are persons who live within a culture, and who, to a greater extent than we realize, are expressions of that culture.

As adolescents engage in faith shaping, there are both interior and external implications. God's transforming presence changes not only the way we believe, feel, and think but also our relationships with others and with society. Young people will have a different relationship to their culture as they encounter transformations in Christ. We will not do justice to adolescents unless we help them consider the shape of their emerging faith in relation to their culture. Ross Snyder has pointed out:

> *Human* beings live in a culture, not just a "natural" world. Each of us is a *self-in-culture*, not just a self. . . . Too long we have acted as if each young person *all by himself* could make up his mind, choose a life style, establish a

life world. If only we poured into him enough facts and admonitions and kept him frantically busy. . . . Actually, he can make up his mind, establish a style of life and life world only *as he is a member of a culture.* . . . Youth is the time to begin . . . creating culture rather than consuming and conforming to the culture other people apart from him make.[1]

Youth are persons-in-culture, and their faith will be more integrative if we enable them to work it out within culture. There is, in contemporary society, a youth culture that is somewhat distinct and identifiable. In part, it is shaped by adolescents themselves, but it is also shaped by the larger society. As young people shape their personal faith, they grow in capacity to be not only recipients of culture but also shapers of it. Faith offers the criteria against which to evaluate one's participation in culture and the courage, when necessary, to be countercultural.

We must confess that as adults we are often insensitive to the ways that culture has compromised our faith and the rare occasions when our faith has prompted us to act counter to popular culture. But in our hearts we can recognize our shortsightedness and cowardice. And if we care about the gospel and about youth, our hope is that they will learn earlier than we did about the relationship between faith and culture.

We are called to affirm that God is at work nurturing and transforming individual persons and human cultures. Our choice is whether we join God in the nurturing and evangelizing tasks with both adolescents and their culture. If we are involved in a ministry with youth, we are, in some small way, shapers of adolescent culture as well as an influence with individual youth.

It was Jesus' desire to evangelize culture. His vision was to evangelize culture by introducing the kingdom of God on earth—*a kingdom culture!* While Jesus advocated preaching the gospel to persons one by one, he talked even more about introducing the kingdom of God in the world.

We are not only to be an influence with youth, but we are to empower them to shape their own culture. We must find ways to affirm those things in adolescent culture that are Christworthy and to suggest alternatives for those things we consider to be destructive. As youth seek our counsel to find legitimate ways in which they can participate in their culture and yet remain faithful to Christ, they are asking an evangelistic question.

Christian youth can be more than consumers. They can be a part of Christ's transforming activity in their culture. The active youth in a

[1]Ross Snyder, *Young People and Their Culture* (Nashville: Abingdon Press, 1969), pp. 35–38.

church spend only a fraction of their time in the church or within its fellowship—maybe no more than four hours a week—yet that time often wields a significant, disproportionate influence in their lives. Because of the nurture we provide, they are often able, in rather remarkable ways, to be strong in the face of evil, to be mature in the face of destructive options, to be responsible about their future in the face of dead ends, and to affirm life as hopeful persons. We are not necessarily asking them to be angry social prophets, confronting their peers in the halls of the school. The quiet, subtle, and humble actions of Christian youth in their culture will often accomplish more than loud demonstrations. Certainly our aim is not to turn young people against their culture, but rather to see it for what it is and to be discriminating in how they are participants in it. The urge to conform to peers is strong in adolescence, and any deviation, based upon quiet but sincere motives, is a significant witness.

What does a culture-shaping witness look like? Traditionally we have asked church-related youth to take negative stands in their culture: not to dance, or smoke, or drink, or take drugs, or have sexual intercourse outside of marriage. We can, however, ask young people to position themselves in their culture in positive ways: to befriend the lonely and ridiculed, to build relationships across racial or ethnic difference, to instigate reconciliation, to represent honesty and truthfulness, to exhibit Christian vocation. As with adults, we can urge Christian youth to participate in their peer culture, to be a part of it, to claim it, and to transform it.

The Task of Culture Shaping

The task of culture shaping with youth involves at least three functions.

The first is to help young people recognize Christ in their culture. The evangelistic task is to point out Christ in other people, in world events, in their own experiences, in their culture. Christ isn't locked up in the church or in stained glass windows or in the private soul of the believer. Christ is already a part of youth culture, and our task is to help youth see Christ there. "The Word had life in himself and this life brought light to men. The light shines in the darkness, and the darkness has never put it out" (John 1:4-5, TEV).

The second function is to help young people shape their culture to be more Christlike. To be merely reluctant recipients of popular culture or to avoid contact with peer culture is not the task of young Christians. An evangelistic question for youth is "How can I make my culture more Christlike?" In the fourth chapter of Luke, Jesus began his public ministry by announcing to the Nazarenes what he intended to do in his Galilean culture: "To announce good news to the poor, to proclaim release for prisoners and recovery of sight for the blind . . ." (Luke 4:18, NEB). When we begin to shape our culture as Christians, these become our goals as well. Justice and liberation become our themes.

The third function is to develop peer ministry in the church as a legitimate, Christ-filled expression of youth culture. Youth culture is not just something "out there," created by disc jockeys and television. It is whatever and wherever youth create it. In your church's peer ministry, do youth claim and recognize the culture that is there as their own, or is it adult-dominated? Youth peer culture expressed in the church can help youth experiment with how to be faithful in today's world.

How to Assist the Task of Culture Shaping

We can now identify some practical ways that adults in the church can support youth as their faith interacts with the culture in which they live.

1. In my church's youth fellowship group, we engage every other year in a project that our youth eagerly anticipate: a youth mission exchange trip. We contact a church within one day's drive and negotiate with them to spend four or five days in their community, and we invite them to spend a similar length of time in our city. The purpose of the exchange trips is for youth to be able to recognize Christ at work in other communities, through another church, through a specific mission project, and through new peer friendships. Instead of engaging in a mission trip in which we go to serve others, we learn through this approach that mission is mutual. Junior high and senior high youth have few opportunities to experience life in new settings in different homes and communities. The newness of the setting makes it easier for them to identify Christ in the community and in people's lives than is possible back home in more familiar settings. In addition they learn a great deal about their own situation when they host the returning group.

2. Another cultural invitation to the gospel can be found in interracial events. We may not always be able to integrate our churches, but we certainly can engage in interracial events with black, white, Hispanic, Asian, and American Indian churches. Through such events we can recognize how Christ works in the world, and we can build bridges of understanding rather than walls of prejudice. I highly recommend bringing two churches together for more than a token, one-time event. Youth from my church and youth from a National Baptist church in our city met for a long-term service project, which concluded with a joint celebration.

3. To the extent that the peer ministry in your church is a legitimate expression by youth of their own youth culture, and to the extent that this youth culture is an expression of Christ, you are extending a cultural invitation to the gospel with youth. If your peer ministry is not Christ-centered but, rather, centered around something more superficial, then there is obvious evangelistic work to be done. If your youth ministry represents adult culture more than that of youth, then you also have an evangelistic task.

The longer I engage in youth ministry, the more convinced I become about the importance of youth providing their own leadership for their activities. I am convinced that the role of the adult in youth ministry is to be an enabler—to help youth do what they choose to do and to be an affirming presence for the youth, as well as for the gospel.

4. Another cultural invitation to the gospel involves the parents of youth. We need to communicate with parents the importance of faith nurturing in the church and in the home. I have, for example, started the tradition of writing a letter to parents of incoming seventh graders, stressing the unique influence they now have to point the attention of their son or daughter to our church's youth ministry. The parents have related to me that this contact helped them to be much more alert and supportive. The pressures on parents are great, and often the reminder is helpful. Faith is the foundation for everything that parents hope will come to their children. Without the foundation of a mature faith, marriages, vocations, skills, friendships, and success will amount to little. Parents do have a cultural contribution to offer to their young people. They can be supportive of peer culture as it occurs in the church, and they can be supportive of their own children as they participate in peer culture in the larger society. But parents need consistent training and support if that is to occur.

5. As we reflect with youth upon their culture, there will be many opportunities in which to discuss questions such as "Where do we see Christ at work in the world? Who or what seems to embody Christ's mission?" In working with individual youth, there will be many opportunities to discuss with them that which is destructive or evil in their culture and ways to make it more Christlike. Many of the moral dilemmas that young people face have this dimension to it. Young people who learn to say no to certain things and yes to other things may by their very response be an influence upon other youth and upon the culture in which they participate. We can train young people to be discerning of Christ in the world and to be discriminating of their culture. We can empower young people

to be not merely consumers but shapers of their culture. In these goals, we need to recognize the courage and difficulty required and be prepared to celebrate "small" victories.

10

Shaping a Nurturing Environment

Let us trust that what we are unable to accomplish with youth, God will accomplish by calling others to join us, both during their adolescent years and beyond. We are summoned to be nurturers and evangels with youth, but we are not called to be their saviors.

In this chapter our focus becomes more practical as we suggest goals for nurturing youth. Specific discipleship programs that can be adapted for use with youth are offered in the appendix of this book.

Nurturing for Transformation's Sake

What do young people need in order to be ready to receive God's transformations? What will be the shape of nurture if its purpose is to prepare young persons for transformation? These are questions too infrequently posed and yet very significant to our nurturing ministry with youth. The fourteen responses below will likely include traditional as well as surprising nurturing activities.

1. Youth need to know how to pray, and not just how to ask God for what they need. Neither youth nor adults in our society have had much experience with quiet and solitude. We are trained to expect little from silence or quiet expectation. Yet prayer is entering into quiet and solitude so that we might receive the presence of the living God. When youth pray, they must be helped not to expect instant gratification, but to expect to understand more deeply God's presence and will.

2. Youth need to trust their intuitions. Youth are taught by our society to trust "the solid facts"—reality that can be objectified or quantified. Yet my most significant discoveries have "come to me" from within rather than resulting from conscious intellectual investigation. Made in God's image, intuition is one of God's most trustworthy gifts. Too often youth will attempt to force an idea or search "out there" for an answer, when by trusting their intuition God's truth comes to them from within.

3. *Youth need to learn to trust their imaginations.* Jesus was an evocative teacher, lifting up images and stories of God's will for human life and stirring the imaginations of his listeners. I have been surprised that as a print-oriented person, I have received God's will most often in visions. For youth, who are more naturally imaginative and culturally much less print-oriented, it is only the adult-world that convinces them that their imaginations are unreliable as a way to seek truth. I have had amazing experiences leading guided meditations with youth in which they relax, close their eyes, and use their imaginations to place themselves inside Scripture's story. They can offer marvelous revelations as they interact with biblical characters and hear "a word" spoken to them.

On one occasion the youth on a retreat planning team decided to set aside one evening for an agape love feast and the Lord's Supper. Two of the most unlikely youth in the group led the entire experience. In a cramped, ugly cabin in the middle of a forest, they invited us to re-enact with our imaginations what happened nearly two-thousand years ago. For several youth the experience resulted in a transforming encounter. The imagination can open us up to the realm of the Holy Spirit.

4. *Youth need to understand what it means to be called or summoned.* God chooses to call young people to a lifetime of faithfulness. Discipleship to Christ is not so much casting about for options, as responding to a call. Youth need to understand that God calls not only pastors but all people. Not only am I called to be a pastor, but my call to be a father was just as moving and identifiable. There are moments when I feel called to do something specific with another person or to respond to some public issue or to say something to a friend in the name of Christ. These need not necessarily be vocational callings, nor even "marker events" in my life, but they are summons to respond to God's will.

5. *Youth need to learn the gift of discernment.* Discernment comes from experience, and in this regard youth are at a disadvantage. My best experience with youth is to develop the gift of communal discernment within an adolescent peer group. Together we can "test the spirit" to see if a vision is in keeping with the vision of the gospel, if an action is consistent with Jesus' ethic, if a call is a summons or merely a self-centered desire. Some of the best learning with youth is in interpreting shared experiences and discovering how we might discern God at work through ourselves and through others.

6. *Youth need to be risk takers.* This is an area where most adolescents can teach adults. Of course, there are some risks worth taking and others not worth taking. The question that must always be asked is "Is the goal worth the risk?" But our God is adventuresome (as evidenced throughout the Bible) and invites us to take risks. As discussed in the first chapter of this book, faith and uncertainty are complementary. If we wait until a risk is minimized, we will likely have missed God's *kairos*, or moment of opportunity.

7. *Youth need to learn mutual accountability.* Jesus warned his disciples that each would have a cross to bear. The summons from God is not to a life of ease, and the joy that God offers will not always appear joyful at first. Within adolescent peer groups or intergenerational groups, we can develop mutual accountability. This involves each person taking responsibility for what others expect of themselves. I cannot decide for you the summons that God has for you. I cannot dictate the direction of your growth. I can listen as you share your responses and decisions and then help you stay on that course. And you can do the same for me, regardless of whether you are an adult or an adolescent.

8. *Youth need to be open to surprise and interruption.* Few people enjoy interruptions. For the most part they appear as a nuisance or distraction from "what we really want to be about." But, my experience has been that God breaks into my consciousness most often as an interruption. Our God is not a god of predictability. God is capable of about-faces, or at least that is what they appear to be to us. When we become open to a God of surprises, surprising transformations can result.

9. *Youth need to develop intimacy within Christian community.* Youth need to encounter intimate community, marked by vulnerability, with their peers as well as with adults. Adolescents have very few places where they can truly be honest with adults without fear of incrimination. Sometimes this can happen with parents, but often not. Occasionally it occurs with teachers or coaches. But it surely needs to occur with adults in the church who have been called to nurture adolescents. Intimacy within the context of Christian community reveals the Christ who is always there in our midst.

10. *We need to bring the traditions of faith near to youth.* Traditions in and of themselves cannot transform or convert. But they can be a marvelous legacy that young people take with them into their adult years. Patterns of nearness, as described in chapter 3, can be used by the Spirit as a future springboard for transformation.

11. *Youth need to see that who they are is a gift, not an individual achievement and not a cruel joke.* Their personhood is a gift from God. The personal resources available to them (their abilities, talents, feelings, thoughts, ideas, visions, skills, dreams, values, personality, physical body, and so forth) are gifts from a loving God whose hope is that they will use these according to a loving Will. When young people see who they are as an achievement, they will question what right God has to enter their lives. If they see who they are as unworthy, they will forever doubt that God would ever want to enter their lives. When they see themselves as valued creations of God, they are more open to transformation.

12. *Youth need to stand alongside the poor, the disenfranchised, the forgotten, the condemned, the lonely, and the imprisoned.* About this the New Testament is very clear: it is in brokenness that we will meet Christ, and it is through "the very least of these" (in the eyes of the world) that God often speaks to us. God is at work in solidarity and transformation at the hurting edges of our lives and of the world, and it is at these places that we can best recognize God's transforming presence.

13. *As adult nurturers we need to model our own experiences of transformation.* We need to be transparent enough so that youth can see how God has acted and is acting within our lives. Of course, there are limits of appropriateness, and all persons need to have privacy. But privacy also has its limits, and there are occasions when we need to share how God's call has entered our lives.

14. *Adult evangelists need to call young people to a point of readiness and celebrate with youth when transformation occurs.* We do not treat the events, professions, and decisions of transformation as celebratively as we might. We need to be sensitively in-tune with youth to know when to call young persons to experiences of transformation.

The Criteria of Nurture

What is being suggested in this chapter is not a program. There may be some techniques to be learned, some new experiences to be gained, some actions to be modeled, or some gifts to be developed. What is suggested is that nurturing for transformation become a new priority that permeates our relationships with youth.

I am not suggesting, and please hear me, that adults be only serious with youth, or that all we ever attempt with youth is to enter into quiet and prayer! *A life lived open to transformation is neither an unnatural one nor a pious one. It is an authentically human life lived in engagement with*

God's world. There are moments for prayer, and let us not miss those. There are moments for play, and let us not miss those either. There are moments for listening, for modeling, for risking, for discernment, for re-creation, and for absence.

But neither let us be deceived about our ultimate goal in ministry with youth. Our ultimate goal is nurture for transformation. We will need to wait for the right opportunities, for God's moments of *kairos*. These can never be forced. But the fact that we have a primary goal does not mean that youth should hear us as broken records, constantly harping on the same theme. It could mean, however, that we examine our ministry with youth and use the criteria of nurturing for transformation as a evaluative guide. Resources are included in the appendix of this book that may be adapted for others committed to nurturing for transformation.

In our ministry with youth we are partners with God in Christ. We can trust that the right opportunities will come along if we are open and ready for them. And finally, let us trust that what we are unable to accomplish with youth, God will accomplish by calling others to join us, both during their adolescent years and beyond. We are summoned to be nurturers and evangels with youth. But we are not called to be their saviors.

11

A Person of Christian Faith

The front side and the back side of the gospel—a free and accountable love—are what it means to be a person of Christian faith today. Young people who begin to grasp this gospel are well on their way to mature faith and fullness of life.

Much of what has been said about the faith nurturing of youth would be applicable to the nurture of any faith, Christian or otherwise, particularly in a pluralistic culture like ours. Young persons growing up in a Buddhist home need faith clarifiers and advocates; they need practices of nearness and directness; they will pass through the same faith-shaping tasks. Faith nurturing of youth is a universal task of all religions.

We, however, want to concern ourselves with the sharing of Christian faith with youth. The quality of faith that young people experience is greatly (though not entirely) influenced by what we as adults and parents extend to them. In a special sense each denomination or church, as a faithful community, must decide for itself what is important to pass along.

This chapter will sketch out the broadest directions in which mature Christian faith travels without attempting to split theological or doctrinal hairs. In the Christian church there is a variety of beliefs, stances, and doctrines. Much of that variety is faithful to Christian experience and to the Scriptures. Much of it stems from a difference in emphasis rather than substance. The variety is one of the things that makes Christianity so universal, creative, and exciting.

What You Believe Matters!

There is in American culture today a nonchalance about faith. There is an "anything goes" mentality. Many people believe that "it doesn't matter what you believe, just as long as you believe in something." "Some-

thing" too often means "anything," and "anything" too often means
"nothing." Some of this mentality reflects a tolerance of the plurality of
faiths that we see exhibited in modern, urban America today. And tolerance toward the faith convictions of others is a good thing. But sloppiness
of conviction is an entirely different matter. Religious traditions and
meanings cannot be served up in a holy smorgasbord so that spiritual
consumers can reach for a bit of this and a bit of that.

Today we seem to lack an authority for belief, a reference point against
which to evaluate positive or negative faith. Orthodoxy is taken to mean
whatever we want or need. It is certainly true that we must personalize
faith. If it is not personalized, then faith is never truly owned. But as
Christians we must ultimately integrate and evaluate our own personal
beliefs (1) against the Scriptures, (2) against the doctrines of our own
faith community, and (3) against the heritage and theology of the universal church.

The doctrine of the priesthood of all believers, held by the free
churches, affirms that no person or hierarchy has authority over the content of another person's faith. It exhibits a tolerance for personal interpretation and individual expression of faith. But this doctrine does not give
persons the *right* to believe whatever they want to believe. Rather, the
emphasis is upon the *responsibility* to interpret faithfully the Scripture.
Many people in the churches have misunderstood the relationship
between right and responsibility.

It does matter who God is to you. It does matter whether faith has
depth. It does matter whether your faith, as I have heard Ernst Campbell
say, "knows the simplicity on the far side of complexity, rather than
becomes satisfied with the simplicity on the near side of complexity." Or,
to repeat the words of Bishop Stephen Neill, the challenge of faith is
always to "commit all that you know of yourself, to all that you know of
God." A faith that is growing and maturing is undoubtedly the strongest
force for good in the world. A faith that is simplistic, naive, or uninformed is dangerous. There are far too many examples of this.

The opposite of faith is not doubt but apathy. Doubt and faith are both
active processes in building a deep and lasting foundation for life. There
is a tug and pull between doubt and faith. Faith satisfies and doubt dis-
satisfies. Faith brings life into perspective, and doubt jostles it out of perspective. Before we allow faith to satisfy at too early or superficial a stage,
doubt is needed to provide the corrective. In a "becoming" Christian,
doubt and faith interplay throughout an entire lifetime.

A typical belief for a junior high Christian might be that God cures illness when you pray. So when her favorite grandmother becomes ill, the young person prays for health and healing. When the grandmother dies, the youth is caught in a faith crisis, often blaming either God or herself. The youth's faith is partially correct: God is involved in life, its healing, and its death. But it is much too simplistic to believe that if we pray, everyone will become well. Such a belief puts us, and not God, in the seat of authority. When doubt is affirmed, the young person can get a better perspective on that belief and eventually deepen her faith. If not, the young person could turn from God as being unfaithful or worry that she did not pray often enough or well enough. Guilt might be carried for years. A faith clarifier could help the young person through doubt and, in doing so, provide a crucial faith-shaping role.

The faith of many youth is joyful, superficial, and emotional. There are appropriate times simply to let them be and let them enjoy that level of "faith-experiencing." The faith they have claimed is not yet ready to be deepened. But there are also times to challenge their faith, to walk with them into creative doubt, and thus deepen the reservoir of their experience, their theology, and their world view.

Doubt is the tool that carries us to the edge of our convictions and to the frontiers of new possibilities. It can be a positive and helpful influence upon our faith. For youth, doubt can often be a corrective to sweeping generalizations, extremism, or simplifications. "Extremism is an inherent danger to the young. When we are young, we get a piece of the truth, and we think we have all the truth. . . . The less we know, the easier it is to convince ourselves that we know everything."[1]

We need both to accept the faith of young people for what it is and to challenge them to greater depths. It is imperative that they feel the acceptance and the challenge together. We must not convey the impression "Your beliefs are not good enough" nor "Your beliefs are sufficient." Rather, we must say, "I affirm where you are spiritually. I encourage you to deepen your faith even more," or "Your faith is fulfilling you now. But look how much more awaits you!"

We need also to note that it is not at all uncommon to find adolescents who enjoy a deep, provocative faith that is vibrant and alive and instigates growth in the adults and youth around them.

The longer young persons freeze faith development at an immature level, the more likely it is that their faith will be discarded in young adulthood or that their level of faith will be arrested and will never plunge to a

[1]William H. Willimon, *The Gospel for the Person Who Has Everything* (Valley Forge: Judson Press, 1978), p. 42.

more mature level.

Sin can be defined as the arrest of our development toward God either in understanding, in our personal will, in our actions, or in our relationship with God. Immature faith not only lacks its own rewards, but it is also against God's will. God created us as becomers, as persons "in search." The apostle Paul says, "Do not be like children in your thinking, my brothers, be children so far as evil is concerned, but be grown up in your thinking" (1 Corinthians 14:20, TEV). Or again, "As a matter of fact, my brothers, I could not talk to you as I talk to people who have the Spirit; I had to talk to you as though you belonged to this world, as children in the Christian faith. I had to feed you milk, not solid food, because you were not ready for it" (1 Corinthians 3:1-2a, TEV).

Criteria of Faith Quality

As we help people grow in faith and as we are concerned (as they are concerned) that their faith be an expression of maturity, we need some criteria against which to evaluate that faith.

I would suggest, as a beginning toward that goal, the following nine statements. If a young person could respond positively to these statements about his or her faith, he or she would have a maturing faith indeed. Areas where a person is less sure would be areas where more reflection is needed.

MY FAITH . . .	DEFINITELY YES				DEFINITELY NO		
1. *is personally satisfying.* (I enjoy it; it's a source of satisfaction.)	1	2	3	4	5	6	7
2. *nourishes me personally and stimulates my growth.* (It's always renewing and challenging me.)	1	2	3	4	5	6	7
3. *offers helpful external resources.* (It brings help to me from the outside; from God, from other people, from the Bible or books, etc.)	1	2	3	4	5	6	7

4. *places me in touch with*   1   2   3   4   5   6   7
others' needs.
(These needs might be
physical, emotional, spiritual.)

5. *makes me able to interpret*   1   2   3   4   5   6   7
life's experiences.
(It helps me understand my
feelings and experiences.)

6. *makes me able to be open*   1   2   3   4   5   6   7
to the new.
(I can face new situations
because of my faith.)

7. *causes me to realize my*   1   2   3   4   5   6   7
personal potential.
(My faith helps me under-
stand my future; to know
my talents and gifts; to
become a better person.)

8. *causes me to be selflessly*   1   2   3   4   5   6   7
humble.
(I think of others first; I
realize my own limita-
tions.)

9. *changes from year to year.*   1   2   3   4   5   6   7
(It grows and deepens as I
become older.)

Another way to evaluate faith would be to describe qualities of immature faith.
IMMATURE FAITH CAN BE CHARACTERIZED BY . . .
   1. *too strong a need for certainty.* Not all questions can be answered;
     the word "faith' implies that one cannot know everything; mature
     faith can live comfortably with some uncertainty.

2. *too small a view of God.* No one can know everything about God or always know God's expectations for one's life; often ideas of God are too small, too limiting, too self-serving.

3. *self-centeredness.* An immature faith seeks only a reward for oneself; centers too exclusively upon one's own personal needs.

4. *it being used as a crutch, an excuse, a comfort.* In all such cases faith gets in the way of personal growth.

5. *a lack of surprises or challenges.* Vibrant faith often makes surprising demands upon one. It confronts where one least expects it.

6. *a one-time faith decision rather than a lifelong journey.* Immature faith lets the believer think that he or she has "made it," that one is on the inside while others are on the outside; it refuses to see faith as a lifelong series of decisions and stages.

7. *a structure of beliefs rather than a responsiveness of faith.* A person holds fast to a set of theological beliefs and thinks of faith as a collection of carefully selected convictions rather than seeing faith as more fluid and dynamic, more responsive to the divine relationship.

8. *a privatized rather than a personalized focus.* A private faith has no interests in being shared with others; a personalized faith is deeply personal, but it is also shared in relationships.

9. *an institutional rather than a corporate concern.* A faith that gives ultimate allegiance to an institution, i.e., a church, is not the same as a faith that binds one to a corporate body of believers.

What Is a Person of Christian Faith?

A person of Christian faith embodies a love that is both free and accountable.

When we first encounter the Christian faith, we experience a love that is freely given—God's grace to us. But as we accept this freely given love, we become aware of another dimension of God's love. We walk around this love and see it from the back. The back side of this free love of God is what God expects of us—accountable love with its responsibilities. As we consider both the front side and the back side of the gospel message, we will recognize ways in which we have distorted this message.

The front side of the gospel message is grace. The headline of our faith is a free, gracious love from God that we do not deserve and cannot earn. This *free love* makes the statement, "I love you regardless of what you do to return my love." When we are loved regardless of the consequences, that love is both free and freeing.

But rather than *love that frees,* most of us satisfy ourselves with *love that cheapens. Cheap love* is superficial love. Jealous and conditional love is cheap love. Relationships where we have to prove ourselves, where we are not valued or prized, are characteristic of love that we feel we must earn—cheap love. We all have so much cheap love in each of our lives that we prize highly those precious few relationships built on the free love that accepts us as we are.

The back side of the Christian message carries the implications of *free love,* that is, *accountable love.* Accountable love is love that cares. Accountable love is a love that motivates us to hold onto one another, to call one another to growth and maturity. Therefore, accountable love renews and vitalizes all of our lives. It is a love with faithfulness, with eternity as the clock that measures its duration. But most of us distort *accountable love* into *careless love,* where nothing is expected and no strings are ever attached. It is love with no requirements—fleeting love— love of the moment. Such a careless love makes no difference and holds no meaning.

If we accept God's *free love,* the implications are that we must enter into a relationship with God that has accountability. We will then be held accountable by God in love.

THE FRONT SIDE OF THE GOSPEL

FREE LOVE VS. CHEAP LOVE

THE BACK SIDE OF THE GOSPEL

ACCOUNTABLE LOVE VS. CARELESS LOVE

When we join together the front side of the gospel, *free love* (love that accepts me as I am), with the back side of the gospel, *accountable love* (love that binds and secures), then we have a *free and accountable love that is the whole of the gospel.* God is calling us to a love that frees, on the one hand, and holds us to our commitments, on the other hand.

But how sad it is that so many of our homes, so many of our families, so many of our churches are built around cheap love on the front side and careless love on the back side. People feel neither accepted nor cared for. Many people do not feel accepted by God because they think only good or better people are really accepted by God. And they are not bound to God because they're frightened of that much responsibility or commitment.

Accountable Love

Our whole society today is running from accountable love—lovers who choose to live together; friends who refuse to challenge one another; parents who won't provide helpful limits for their children; or church members who shy from commitment. We appear absolutely enamored with *careless love!* We don't want to inconvenience anyone; we don't want to make mutual demands upon anyone; we don't want to place expectations in anyone's path.

The younger generation is frequently charged with shirking accountability. But this problem does not belong only to those on the high school or college campus. Those of us in the pulpit and pew and those of today's older generation are just as guilty. Anytime I hear a senior adult say that he or she is too old to sit in the crib room and hold a baby or that he or she has taken a turn with the second graders and now it's someone else's turn, that reason alone suggests careless love. Whenever I see someone who lives in a lovely home, with lovely cars and the nicest clothes, but not sharing a sacrificial percentage of her or his income toward helping others, I know I'm seeing a person caught up by the grip of careless love. We are all guilty—it is symptomatic of our age.

Accountable love is perhaps more difficult to comprehend. Let me use an illustration from my own ministry with youth. Accountable love was the unexpected "theme" of one youth retreat.

I had taken a group of youth to a lodge that was in a remote location. At 10:00 P.M. the second night out, two boyfriends unexpectedly drove up to meet two girl friends who were in the senior high group. And we had an instant problem! The boys had graduated from high school six months before. During high school they had been an active part of our youth fellowship group. But these capable young men, in all ways able to enter the adult world, seemed stalled in their willingness to face the post-high-school decisions of life.

The counselors huddled soon after their arrival to decide what to do. What was the loving thing to do? If we let them stay overnight, we would not be encouraging their forward momentum to maturity. If we sent them home, we would no doubt anger the girls and the boys.

Accountability was really the question. Should we risk anger, alienation, and misunderstanding? Was it more important to hold them accountable for their own actions? For me, the issue was really even more complicated than that. I had played the role of close friend and near-father to these boys. For five years I had appreciated and enjoyed their friendships. I knew that if I sent them home, my contact with them and their relationship with the church might come to an end. My own feelings and emotions were involved.

Midnight rolled around and the boys were not moving. The adults finally had to take action. We decided to take the risk and hold the boys accountable for their actions. How painful it was for me to see the looks on their faces, not only that night, but for weeks and months to come, of surprise, of distrust, of hurt, and of anger! They wondered out loud, "How can a friend of ours treat us this way? How can you kick us out?" I wondered back, out loud, "How can someone who loves you treat you any other way?"

In the cab of a pickup truck at three in the morning with a blizzard of snow falling about us, I shared with them my disappointment during the past six months and my strong belief in their future if they would believe in it themselves. I can only hope that someday they will look back on that occasion and thank a group of adults who loved them enough to hold them accountable. Lesser love would have found an easier solution.

In the short run it *appears* much easier to be friends without holding one another mutually accountable. It *appears* much easier to rear your children without truly holding them accountable. It *appears* easier to be in a church that cannot or will not hold you accountable. And it is certainly much easier to follow a "god" who does not seem to hold you accountable.

In the story of Ananias and Sapphira in Acts they, too, thought it to be much easier to avoid accountability.

They were a part of the first Christian community. The members of this community entered a covenant with their God. They were to be loyal to God, and God was to be loyal to them. It was a mutual vow of accountable love. This first church felt led of God to establish that if any member sold a property, the proceeds of that property would be given to the church so that the common ministry could be furthered. But Ananias decided to go only halfway. He sold his property and gave only part of it to the church. He and his wife kept back the rest. They broke the church's covenant. In this story we often get overly concerned with their punishment. Both of them denied their wrongdoing, and both of them came under conviction and fell over dead. But we miss the real point when we accent the punishment. The point is, rather, that the early church expected that their love for each other and for God would be an accountable love, love filled with enough concern and seriousness that it would be binding, not a casual or flippant love. The story is not about the cruelty of their punishment but of the seriousness of the church's love.

In healthy circumstances, to be held accountable means that someone will help me keep my life on the track that I have chosen. Mutual accountability with a group means that together we are going to be responsible to keep our common goals on target.

We use the words "*holding* another person accountable," and there's something very loving about holding another person. When we take someone into our arms, when we hold, touch, embrace, reach out to another—these are expressions of love.

Indeed to care enough in a loving relationship to hold someone accountable reflects a love that is deep, abiding, and true. A group of people, if they are truly serious with one another, will hold one another accountable in love.

One of the most important persons in my life was a man named Mr. Ward. Mr. Ward was a speech and drama teacher in my high school. He was the town philosopher and the village radical in my little community in central Missouri.

Few men have had more impact upon my life. He would start every semester with a new class by scaring the wits out of us with all the commitments and expectations that he had for us. He would tell us how seriously he would hold us accountable. And he would end the class by saying that if anyone felt he or she could not live up to the expectations, the person should get up and leave. But then he would say, "But if you really want to be challenged, if you truly want to think, then I'll promise all my efforts to that end." No one would ever leave the class.

And Mr. Ward followed up on his promise. He truly cared about his students. He cared about our troubles that had nothing to do with speech or drama. I can still remember him saying to me on numerous occasions, "Steven, I believe in you. I count on you." And through his love, I felt free to think and grow as I had never done before.

Mr. Ward's love and accountability were a great deal like the accountable love that God has for us. Yes, we're challenged and frightened with the expectations that God has for us. Yet God doesn't force us to accept such love. God offers it. God is saying to us, "If you decide to enter into covenant with me, to be my faithful people in your homes, with your children, in your work, with your friends, in your school—wherever you might be, your life will take on a richer meaning that you cannot now imagine. You will taste freedom. You will be taking my love as seriously as I am taking you."

That is God's promise to us.

Free Love

What a gift—what an incredible gift is God's free love! Just as parents love their child regardless of whether the child returns the love or regardless of the child's actions or behavior, so much more does our heavenly Parent love us, regardless of whether we love back or whether we deserve the love.

A love that can freely accept or a love that we must earn—that is the choice which Jesus clearly offers. Each love had its own ethic. The ethic of grace is an ethic of natural response because our actions are in response to God's first action toward us. "We love because he first loved us."

The ethic of a love which we must earn is an ethic of achievement. Our actions are intended to achieve a certain status with God. We act in order to please, in order to gain acceptance. Many Christians have never fully realized the extraordinary difference which the reality of grace can make. Grace should be the first chapter of the faith which we advocate to youth. It is the reality most suited to their developmental needs.

ETHIC OF RESPONSE	ETHIC OF ACHIEVEMENT
(We love because God first loved us.)	(We love in order to gain status with God.)
Motivation: Gratitude	*Motivation: Obligation*
We act regardless of whether we win or lose.	We act in order to get results, to be successful or victorious.
We serve because we know that we are loved and accepted.	We serve in order to gain love and acceptance.
We aim toward doing the maximum.	We aim toward doing the minimum.

Summary

There is no gospel that young people need to hear more clearly than the gospel of a free and accountable love. We have too exclusively taught youth that everything they want in life they must earn. There is one thing in life that they do not have to earn and cannot possibly earn, and that is God's love (Ephesians 2:8-9). God loves each young person regardless of what a person does or does not do in return. Each is accepted just as each one is. What good news that is for an adolescent: to be thoroughly and unconditionally accepted—by God, no less!

But that is only half the picture. Youth also need to know of God's accountable love. They need to know that God wants to enter into a relationship that will be taken seriously. It will be a relationship where promises are taken seriously, where *they* as persons are taken seriously. They will come to know that God has great hopes and a tremendous purpose for their lives. And that, in love, God will hold them accountable for what they make of life's possibilities.

The front side and the back side of the gospel—a free and accountable love—are what it means to be a person of Christian faith today. Young people who begin to grasp this gospel are well on their way to mature faith and fullness of life.

Jesus is the example of that kind of love incarnated. Through his life we can see a human example of a free and accountable love at work. Yet most children and youth of the church have an almost nonexistent sense of Jesus' humanity. In liberal and conservative churches alike, we pour layers of doctrine and theology over Jesus' humanity as to make him barely distinguishable. We so stress the divine, sinless, perfect, meek, and mild Lord of faith that our young people have no knowledge of the earthy, troubled, worried, joyful, caring, revolutionary Jesus of history.

It is the *man* that youth should see first. Let them come to know Jesus as a person who treated women as equals, who lost his cool in the temple, who humbled himself to wash the feet of others and who exalted himself on Palm Sunday, who celebrated with wine at a wedding, who played with children, who disobeyed his parents at age twelve, who was frightened in Gethsemane, who offended his townspeople in Nazareth, and who held intimate friendships with Mary, Martha, and Lazarus. Let them see Jesus as a man first!

Then, we can interpret to them the role Jesus played in history, the special idea of incarnation and the new relationship made possible with God for each of us. We need more of a beginnings approach to Jesus and less of a basics style.

Youth need to identify with Jesus. They need to feel his feelings with him; to walk his steps with him; to identify with his words and thoughts; to watch him as he grew! When they meet this Jesus, they will meet a compelling and appealing expression of free and accountable love in raw flesh and real blood!

12

A New Mandate!

The challenge of faith shaping with youth remains a diffused agenda in far too many homes and churches. Let us not avoid what is intangible just because it cannot be easily seen or scientifically charted. From Hebrews we are reminded, "Faith is the substance of things hoped for, the evidence of things not seen" (11:1, KJV). Following this biblical advice, we need to help youth discover the very substance of their hopes!

The act of welcoming youth into the faith deserves our most creative and determined response. We must not be guilty of forcing faith upon youth, but, rather, we must surround them with positive faith-shaping experiences in a variety of settings of their lives.

The task of faith shaping by persons in their adolescent and young adult years is sacred and holy. We must allow it to happen along God's timetable. Our efforts will, it is hoped, transmit an enticement toward faith and not anxiousness about faith.

Although it has not been stated as such, this is without apology a book on personal evangelism. It expresses an evangelistic concern to share faith with adolescents and young adults.

This approach has attempted to overcome the two ways we have often exclusively expressed our evangelistic concern for youth. This exclusivity is reflected when we care only for the first-time decision of faith and not the lifelong journey of faith. Second, it is reflected when evangelism is narrowly defined as an activity of directness but not also of nearness.

If we are to speak an inclusive evangelistic message to the youth in our homes and churches, then the "words" we use will have to be EMBODIED WORDS as well as SPOKEN WORDS. We will have to live the message as well as verbalize it. We will need to be more concerned that youth come to *their* own saving knowledge of Christ than to *our* saving knowledge of Christ.

We are challenged in both the Old and New Testaments with a significant mandate to share the precious "words" of faith with our youth.
Hear now these words of Scripture:

THE OLD TESTAMENT MANDATE FOR FAITH NURTURING

"Israel, remember this! The Lord—and the Lord alone—is our God. Love the Lord your God with all your heart, with all your soul, and with all your strength. Never forget these commands that I am giving you today. *Teach them to your children and youth.* Repeat them when you are at home and when you are away, when you are resting and when you are working. Tie them on your arms and wear them on your foreheads as a reminder. Write them on the doorposts of your houses and on your gates.

"In times to come your *children and youth* will ask you, 'Why did the Lord our God command us to obey all these laws?' Then tell them, 'We were slaves of the king of Egypt, and the Lord rescued us by his great power. With our own eyes we saw him work miracles . . .'" (Deuteronomy 6:4-9, 20-22a, TEV; the term "children" is made inclusive of youth in the two italicized sections by the author).

When young persons eventually ask, at their point of readiness, "Why does God call us to faith?" answer them not with doctrine or creed, but share with them the story of our faith and the story of our biblical heritage. Show them God acting in human lives, interrupting history with divine loving concern. Through these stories they will most fully come to faith.

THE NEW TESTMENT MANDATE FOR FAITH NURTURING

"If our gift be the stimulating of the faith of others let us set ourselves to it" (Romans 12:8a, Phillips).

Young persons today, as much as ever before, need gifted and committed persons who see as their calling the nurturing of the adolescent faith journey.

The work of this book can only be a beginning, a send-off, a challenge, a mandate! Now, as these pages come to an end, our real "work" begins as we commit ourselves anew to create the environment, establish the priorities, and develop the relations that will authentically speak God's evangelistic message of concern to young persons.

If we give adolescent faith nurturing our finest efforts and most prayerful concern, then persons of mature Christian faith will emerge. And when our young people receive and shape such a faith, we will be living our finest hour!

Appendix
Resources for Nurturing

Resource #1

A Christian Discipleship Journey for Junior High Youth

For eleven years I have used an approach for discipleship with youth that has been adapted by the three different churches that I have served and by other churches who have learned of it. During the first three years of my pastoral ministry, I attempted to follow the more traditional approach of an annual membership (or confirmation) class during the Lenten season. As pastor, I was the sole adult responsible for telling the youth the pertinent information that they would need to know to make a decision about Jesus Christ. With each group I sincerely tried not to apply any pressure but attempted to communicate the freedom of each adolescent to confront this decision in his or her own time. But, regardless of my effort, the conclusion of these sessions was inevitably viewed as a time of "graduation." The seventh-graders had all taken the course, and baptism (confirmation) was the graduation ceremony. To have not responded was to view oneself as a failure. Besides, if you "flunked," you ran the risk of having to take the class over again! Worse, with both parents and youth, there was a real sense that once the "diploma" was in hand, the struggle was over, and all could sigh with relief. My struggle had just begun! It was my perspective that baptism (confirmation) marked the beginning of the personal faith pilgrimage; but the model we were using and the assumptions which accompanied it communicated exactly the opposite. To make matters even more problematic, because the pastor was the only adult involved in the class, we communicated that only a "professional" could bear an adequate witness as to the truth of what the young people were learning.

Three years was enough. I was determined to find a better way. The three churches I have pastored have been unique from one another, yet I have encountered the same mind-set in each church. The following proposal has been well received in all three contexts, though it was obviously individualized by each congregation to suit its own needs.

When the model was first developed, we determined that its approach must be more interactive in terms of adults and youth together. We wanted the interaction to be a partnership, with youth experiencing adults in their own faith pilgrimage as well as the other way around. We determined that no longer could our concentrated focus upon discipleship with youth be a one-time class. In fact, we determined that "class" was the wrong approach. A discipleship emphasis should occur annually with all youth, regardless of whether or not they had been baptized or confirmed. We decided, for developmental purposes, that a junior high model should be distinct from a senior high model. In particular we wanted the junior high model to be more active and experiential, without compromising the integrity of their encounter with Christian tradition. Finally, we decided that the responses and decisions of young people to faith in Jesus Christ are utterly unique. We must trust that God is at work, and in God's own time the nurture and evangelism in which we are engaged will bear fruit. When a response or decision is made, the church must welcome each one in celebration of who the young person is and of the unique nature of his or her decision. We recognized that an initial decision was merely that and should not be judged by "adult" criteria, nor should the adolescent be required to explain it in adult terminology.

The Junior High Discipleship Journey

In January and February of each year, our youth ministry focuses upon discipleship with youth. For five weeks the junior high youth engage in a discipleship journey in which they choose one destination. The model offered here is designed for an American Baptist church, but churches from other denominations could easily adapt the destinations and the projects.

There are four destinations, and during the three years of junior high school, adolescents choose three of the destinations. We feel that choice is absolutely crucial. The four destinations are: *Bible and Belief, the Local Church, Serving and Caring,* and *Baptists and Heritage.* In each destination there are projects to be accomplished within the five weeks. Some projects are required and others are optional.

We ask each junior high youth to enter the journey with one parent, and we recruit additional adults for those youth whose parents are unavailable or uncomfortable with this request. At an initial dinner we ask the youth to pair themselves with someone else's parent, not their own. This adult-youth pair remains together throughout the five weeks. We've found the adults to be highly motivated, for they want their own adolescent to have as good an experience with another parent. Friendships have emerged from these intergenerational partnerships.

We have found in one evening that we can interpret the model, pair the parents and youth, ask the adult partners to assist the youth as they select destinations, decide upon the optional projects, obtain the necessary resources (all available that evening), and think about a time line for completing the projects within the five weeks. All of that can be accomplished within seventy-five to ninety minutes. No pastor or youth group leader makes decisions for the partners. We stress that the exploration is satisfactory as long as the two of them are comfortable with the decisions that they have made and with the responses by the young person. We stress that this is a journey, a time of exploration, and not merely "work." Certainly, it is not busywork. In each destination there obviously must be reading to do and thoughtful reflection, but we have attempted to find as many active and experiential ways to explore each destination as possible. We realize that junior high youth learn best by doing and then reflecting upon their action.

We hold the initial planning sessions on a Friday evening so that the youth (along with youth group sponsors) can go on an overnight retreat. On this retreat we focus for several hours on some aspect of discipleship. We also allow for a large span of recreational time to balance the remainder of the program.

Halfway through the journey, the third Sunday, we have a thirty-minute work session so that adult partners and youth can strategize together as to the remaining projects to be completed. On the final Sunday we ask a deacon of the church to meet with each youth/adult team during the church school hour. The purpose of this session is for young persons to realize that some adult leader in the church has indeed heard them tell of their experience, reflected together upon its meaning, and affirmed their effort. It is not a moment to pass judgment or even to correct. This is the moment for a faith clarifier.

Following the session, the young people are recognized before the entire congregation. They are given certificates, and each young person displays some of his or her projects. We consider this an important event in the church's calendar and a special moment of congregational celebration. The adult partners are also recognized.

In the following section you will find the Christian Discipleship Journey information packet given to junior high youth and their partners and a design for a three-hour Saturday morning retreat session with the junior high youth. These models may help you plan a similar journey for your junior high youth.

Christian Discipleship Journey
The First Baptist Church,
Dayton, Ohio
. . . INFORMATION SHEET . . . Junior High Youth

DO YOU WANT TO GO ON A JOURNEY???
*Who wouldn't? Everyone enjoys journeys and trips, particularly to faraway
or unusual places . . . like Hawaii, or Disney World, or Europe, or Hong
Kong, or . . . well, you could let your mind run wild with the excitement of a
long journey!*

The Christian Discipleship Journey is an exciting journey, too! It will be a
journey where you can also travel great distances, but not in miles. This is
a journey with your life: to discover what *possibilities for you* there are in
the Christian life!

You will find yourself in the midst of all kinds of experiences on this journey, but it's like any other journey: if you don't jump into it completely, you
probably won't enjoy yourself. (Hawaii wouldn't be much fun if you just sat
in your hotel room!) When you decide to take this journey, make certain it
is your choice and your decision. Make certain you want to discover some
answers to this question:

Am I ready to consider the Christian journey for my life?

This journey is for all junior high youth. Your decision to be baptized or to
join the church is not really dependent on this journey, although what you
learn here should help you down the road of Christian discipleship, and it
might help you make the important decision of accepting God into your
life.

If you are interested, study the covenant and information enclosed. We're
just about to pack up and begin!

ROAD MAP

Just like any trip, you're going to have to know what to plan for and how
and where you're going to travel. Here's a Road Map for the Christian
Discipleship Journey:
   1. *One parent (or substitute) accompanies each young person in the
      journey.*
   2. *Each young person is teamed with one parent (not one's own), and
      these teams are partners for the journey.*
   3. *Each adult-youth team "covenants" to arrive at one of the destina-
      tions of the journey by February 10.*
   4. *In each destination there will be some required and some optional
      projects. The projects must be the work of the youth, but the adults
      are to be supportive in the completion of each project. Projects that*

have an askerisk (*) beside them are projects in which two or more youth in the journey can work together.
5. *You will be given folders in which to record your progress and reactions.*

Overall Requirements for All Journeyers

(1) Attend the overnight retreat without parents. This is a concept-building session on the discipleship concepts of "belonging" and "believing," especially designed for junior high youth.
(2) Attend the work session, at midpoint in the journey, with your adult partner, and attend a Review Session with your adult partner and a deacon on the last day of the journey.

Schedule of Group Gatherings for the Journey

Friday, January 4,	6:00 P.M.	Youth and Parents' Dinner and Organizational Meeting
	8:00 P.M.	Youth only leave for Camp Kirkwood overnight retreat
Saturday, January 5,	5:00 P.M.	Youth return to the church
Sunday, January 27,	12:30 P.M.	Light lunch at church after church school Youth and Parent Partners' Work Session: midway point
Sunday, February 10,	11:15 A.M.	Youth and Parent Partners each meet privately with one deacon to review completed work and affirm the journey
	12:30 P.M.	Congregational recognition of youth who have completed their destination; presentation of Christian Discipleship Journey certificates

Destination: Bible and Belief

REQUIRED:

1. Read our new Church Covenant. In your own words, tell how the covenant reflects the beliefs of church members.
2. Lead your family in daily devotions for one week using *The Secret Place,* a small magazine available at the church.
3. Interview your adult partner on the meaning of prayer in his/her life. Write down five questions you wish to ask and record the answers.

OPTIONALS:
(Choose 2)

1. Create a Bible story pantomime or skit for a group of junior highs to perform during the church school hour for another class. Selection of this Bible story should be coordinated with the teacher.
2. Read *Pilgrim's Progress,* written by an early Baptist pastor, John Bunyan, and answer questions related to the book on Sheet B.
3. Memorize Matthew 5:1-12 or 1 Corinthians 13.
4. Write a short paper on the "Five Identifying Marks" of a Christian. Base this on your own opinion.
5. Read Matthew 4:23–5:16 in each of the following translations: *The Living Bible, The New English Bible,* Today's English Version, the King James Version, and the Revised Standard Version. Write on a sheet or record on a tape recorder what you think this passage is saying and your reactions from reading it in the different translations.

Destination: Serving and Caring

REQUIRED:

* 1. Complete two hours in mission to the community through projects of the Community Mission committee of our Board of Mission.
2. Visit one "shut-in" church member in that person's home or a nursing home, and take something that you have made to affirm that you care, such as cookies, a potted plant, a card, a craft item.
3. Recycle cans, glass, newspaper, and aluminum in your home for three weeks and deliver items to a recycling center, or spend two hours on a litter hike in your neighborhood.

OPTIONALS:
(Choose 2)

* 1. Complete one project from the Service Projects booklet of the American Baptist Churches, U.S.A.
2. Do some research and write a two-page report about a famous Christian (for example, Martin Luther King, Jr., Albert Schweitzer, Tom Dooley, Helen Barrett Montgomery, Ann and Adoniram Judson).

3. Accompany the deacons as they serve Communion in homes to shut-ins on one Sunday afternoon.
4. Find three Bible verses that encourage God's people to care for the world, to be good stewards of what God has given us. Select one of these verses that would make an attractive "paper banner." You can get a long roll of paper from the church, and use felt-tip pens or tempera paint.

Destination: Baptists and Heritage

REQUIRED:

* 1. Attend one other American Baptist church for worship.
* 2. Attend a church of another denomination for worship one Sunday.
3. Read the book *The New Life* by Allan R. Knight and Gordon H. Schroeder. Answer the questions at the end of each study.
4. Read *The Story of American Baptists* (L515-430). What are some of your thoughts about Baptist history?

OPTIONALS:
(Choose 1)

1. Write a letter to one American Baptist international missionary telling him/her who you are, about your discipleship journey, and offering a short prayer for his or her work.
2. American Baptists have two ordinances: baptism and Communion. Using resource books, answer these questions:
Where did baptism begin? When do Baptists baptize people? What is our form of baptism called? Why do we baptize in the way that we do? What do we think that baptism means? What are other forms of baptism that other churches use?
Why do we celebrate the Lord's Supper? Where did this practice begin? What do the bread and the juice symbolize? What is the symbolism of "sitting at the table of the Lord"? According to American Baptists, who can sit at the Lord's table?
3. Make a time line tracing the beginning of the Baptist denomination, ending with the present-day American Baptist Churches, U.S.A.

4. Make a large poster stating the major beliefs of Baptists.

Destination: The Local Church

REQUIRED:

1. Complete the Pledge Card and turn it in if you haven't.
* 2. Attend the January 30 annual meeting of the congregation.
3. Complete the Christian Stewardship Audit based upon your lifestyle. Write a short prayer on the back side based upon the signs in your life of being God's steward.
4. Read the booklet "A Sesquicentennial History of First Baptist Church, Dayton, Ohio" and answer related questions on Sheet G.

OPTIONALS:
(Choose 3)

* 1. Attend the Martin Luther King, Jr., Community Birthday Observance worship service on Tuesday, January 15, 7:30 P.M. Answer related questions on Sheet H.
2. Write a prayer that you will give as the invocation in a worship service on Sunday.
3. Memorize our church covenant.
4. Create a bulletin board in one of the children's church school classes based on a theme they are currently studying.
5. Interview a longtime church member and write a one-page description of his or her experiences within our church.
6. Help in a children's church school class for two Sundays.
7. Take pictures (you may borrow the church's Polaroid from the Resource Center if you need it) of scenes around the church depicting:
    —the church at play
    —the worshiping church
    —the church where people pray
    —the singing church
    —the church, a place to learn
    —the church for all ages
    On poster paper, mount these pictures with their captions.

The Youth Ministry Committee is responsible for administering the Christian Discipleship Journey. Deacons will review the progress of each participant and give congregational recognition for those who complete their stage of the Journey.

A CERTIFICATE OF RECOGNITION

On this day, _____, 19____, the First Baptist Church of Dayton, Ohio,

recognizes _____ for completing work on this destination in the Discipleship Jour-

ney: _____. The congregation lifts up this young person for the interest and

commitment evident in reaching this destination.

_____
(adult partner)

_____
(pastor)

_____
(chairperson, youth ministry)

"Speaking the truth in love,
we are to grow up in every way . . . .
into Christ . . ." (Ephesians 4:15).

Instructions for Deacons Who Are Meeting with Junior High Youth in the Discipleship Journey

1. Each youth, assisted by an adult partner, has worked for five weeks doing required and optional work in one of four "destinations." The destinations in the journey are Bible and Life, the Local Church, Baptist and Heritage, and Serving and Caring.

2. You will meet with one team (one youth and one adult partner). Prior to this meeting you do not need to know anything specific about the nature of this discipleship journey. It will be good for the young person to explain it to you.

3. Your responsibility is to be a good listener, to ask questions of explanation, and to assist the young person in clarifying his or her own faith position. Ask questions that will prompt the young person to verbalize what the journey meant and what he or she has learned.

4. The role of the deacon is neither to judge nor correct nor evaluate. Your presence will communicate to the young person that someone in the church cares about what he or she has done and wants to affirm him or her. As long as the destination has been completed to the satisfaction of the youth/adult team, it deserves your affirmation and the church's recognition.

5. This is likely a nervous moment for the youth. Your informal and friendly response will mean a great deal to him or her.

Thanks so much for your role in the Christian Discipleship Journey!

The Junior High Overnight Discipleship Retreat

The overnight retreat is mostly a time of group building and relaxation. As we arrive on Friday evening, we often do an affirming exercise to recognize the giftedness of each participant. The remainder of the evening is for group games and informal fellowship.

We do plan three hours on Saturday morning for the young people to reflect more specifically on the nature of a faith decision. The model we have frequently used allows the young people to search actively for their own answers. In essence, we set up informal learning centers in the retreat lodge: a reading corner that includes brief excerpts from appropriate books that are of interest to junior high youth; a listening center that features tapes of several contemporary parables; a Scripture corner that suggests texts in modern translations; and a discussion center.

We have repeated this particular design for several years, changing the materials in each center. Other years we have used a film or a different model.

When we use the learning center approach, we distribute the following handout to the youth and urge them to choose one of the three questions to answer. They complete the six responses by going to the various centers in the room at their own pace and in the order of their choice.

A time of group sharing concludes the morning.

Handout
Christian Discipleship Journey Retreat . . . .
Junior High Youth

Choose One Question to Explore:
A. What does it mean to trust God?
B. What is a personal faith?
C. What does God expect of us?

Answer That Question by . . .

1. INTERVIEWING (Ask that question of the two persons on this retreat and write down their answers.)

2. READING (Go to the Reading Corner, read the articles or the books, and jot down some responses here.)

3. PERSONALIZING (Answer the question from your own experience.)

4. LISTENING (Go to the Tape Recorder Corner and play the tape related to your question. On the tape is a modern parable. The questions at the end of the tape will help you relate it to your subject. One question has a cartoon booklet rather than a recording.)

5. GOING TO SCRIPTURE (Go to the Scripture Corner and look up related passages. Record your ideas here.)

6. DISCUSSING (With others working on the same question, share your insights and learnings and record here.)

Resource #2

The Senior High Overnight Discipleship Retreat

We recognize that a different model is needed for senior high youth, though it is built upon many of the same assumptions as the junior high retreat. For the older youth, an overnight retreat is the focus of the experience. Each young person is asked to invite an adult to be a partner on this retreat. We urge that these partners be neither parents nor their youth group sponsors. What has intrigued me over the years is how rarely an adult has turned down the request of a senior high youth to be his or her partner. It has been, for nearly all the adults, a real affirmation to have been invited to participate.

For these youth, the retreat is a highly concentrated time. We have planned it, for convenience sake, on the same weekend as the junior high overnight retreat, with the younger youth departing late Saturday afternoon and the senior high youth and adult partners arriving early Saturday afternoon. The time together on Saturday afternoon is recreational time. Once the junior high youth depart, the remainder of the retreat is devoted to reflecting upon the question "Where am I in my discipleship journey?" Some youth will have yet to be baptized or confirmed, and yet the question is still relevant for them. We stress at the beginning of this retreat that the question is directed to adults as well as youth. The adult/youth teams are truly partners, and we anticipate that youth are present to be a resource for the adults as well as the other way around. I have witnessed more mutuality across intergenerational lines on this retreat than anywhere else in my ministry with youth. Friendships that have emerged have lasted for years. We urge the youth to invite a different adult each year, so the possibility exists of a senior high youth having three different adult partners.

We have developed three retreats so that a young person will not experience repetition during his or her high school years. What follows is the design we have used for one of these retreats. (We have used the "Criteria of Faith Quality" found in the chapter "A Person of Christian Faith" as the basis for a second retreat design with the senior high youth.)

Discovering My Vocation

This three-hour exercise entitled "Discovering My Vocation" gives participants an opportunity to gain greater clarity about the vocation to which God is calling them. It is not designed necessarily for those seeking career changes. Rather, it defines vocation broadly. Youth *have* vocations and are not merely awaiting them. Contrary to the customary approach, this exercise identifies gifts by first asking participants to identify nine primary characteristics of their lives (what they enjoy most, important involvements, relationships, commitments). Then participants are asked to identify personal gifts that seem to be evidenced in the characteristics. From these gifts, the exercise leads participants through prayer, meditation, and biblical reflection to answer three specific questions about the vocation to which they feel called by God.

The result is not necessarily a new or different vocation, but greater clarity and insight into their gifts and vocations.

(The exercise can also be used with a large group of participants by dividing them into small groups of two to five participants.)

The exercise begins with a process of identifying gifts. For this exercise, the word "gifts" will be used in its broadest meaning: the talents, abilities, and personal resources that God has given each person (see chapter 7). By identifying their gifts, the participants have greater clarity as they confront the vocation to which God calls them. Allow up to three hours.

In addition to the following worksheets, you will need to provide five blank cards in these three colors: yellow, brown, and blue. The cards should fit within the boxes on worksheet 2 of the exercise. (Most printing companies throw away card stock in this small size. Or, colored index cards or construction paper can be used.)

Distribute worksheets 1 and 2 and the cards to each participant. Allow twenty-five minutes for the participants to write on the yellow, brown, and blue cards as described on the bottom of worksheet 1. Then, ask the participants to prioritize these cards in terms of their personal importance, placing their most important commitment in the box marked #1 in the blue card column, and so forth.

Distribute worksheet 3. Ask the participants to place the top three cards in each color randomly down the left hand side of worksheet 3. After the nine cards have been moved to worksheet 3, ask the participants to examine these traits. If some seem repetitive, replace one or more cards with a fourth priority from worksheet 2. You might point out that for the purpose of this exercise, these nine traits have been identified. Obviously our lives are much more complex than the nine traits could possibly reflect.

Now they are to identify their gifts by matching the traits on the left with the list of gifts on the right, drawing lines to connect them. Match no more than two gifts to each trait.

You may want to ask participants to circle newly recognized gifts. Urge participants to add gifts at the bottom of the right column as necessary. Allow twenty minutes.

Distribute worksheet 4. By this time participants have identified some of their gifts. God has purposely given us gifts to be used in the vocation to which we are called. Allow ten to fifteen minutes for the participants to examine the two biblical references that offer criteria for discerning God's will.

Next, the adult-youth partners will share the results of their work on worksheet 3 and probe together God's will for their lives. This will take twenty to thirty minutes.

At least ten minutes will be needed to allow partners to look again with their imaginations over their gifts on worksheet 3. As they see these gifts, they may see ways to use them in ministry. Stress the importance of the imagination in seeing new possibilities and hearing the Spirit.

Finally, allow five minutes for silent and personal prayer. Leaders might begin this time by reverently reading the scriptural passage on the bottom of worksheet 5. Prayer is listening as well as speaking or asking. Urge the participants to be receptive as God leads them in prayer.

Allow up to twenty-five minutes to complete the exercise on worksheet 5 by responding to the three questions in section VIII.

The partners can share section VIII with each other and close with intercessory prayer.

Discovering My Vocation
Worksheet 1

"Ministry is not so much what you do, but how you approach what you do; ministry is a vocation."   (Carolyn Mac-Dougall)

Ministry is a life of faithfulness to God, not a profession alongside other professions."   (Veegie Short)

"Each person is born with potential. In the community of faith, this potential is nurtured to reveal actual talents for ministry. When these talents are surrendered to God, they become spiritual gifts empowered by the Holy Spirit for use in some specific vocation or ministry."   (Veegie Short)

"It is important to us as individuals, and for the church as a supportive community, to embrace the diversity of each of our unique experiences, skills, to help us sort out our own 'rough draft' theologies for daily living, to help us develop a stronger sense of self and purpose in defining our own vocations, and to help each of us to be as fully 'present' in the world as we can."   (Carolyn Mac-Dougall)

KEY
QUESTIONS

● 1. What is my God-given vocation in life?
● 2. How can I transform my relationships, responsibilities, involvements, and gifts into a ministry for God?
● 3. What are God's callings and purposes for my life?

DIRECTIONS:

I. On five yellow cards, list five things you enjoy most.

   On worksheet 2, place these cards in priority of importance to you, the most important in box number 1, etc.

II. On five brown cards, list five relationships or involvements that best express who you are.

   On worksheet 2, prioritize these in the boxes provided. Then return to this sheet and the next exercise.

III. On five blue cards, list five commitments you have made that play a significant role in your life.
   On worksheet 2, prioritize these in the boxes provided.

IV. Take the top three cards in each of three columns on worksheet 2 and place them in random order on the left side of worksheet 3. In what ways do these traits reflect your gifts? Match the items in the left column with the gifts listed in the right column, adding other gifts at the bottom. (Draw lines to connect cards on the left to gifts on the right.)
   The gifts that God has given you are undoubtedly expressed within the things you enjoy most, your relationships, involvements, and commitments.

Worksheet 2

FIVE THINGS YOU ENJOY MOST (yellow cards)	FIVE INVOLVE-MENTS/RELATION-SHIPS THAT BEST EXPRESS WHO YOU ARE (brown cards)	FIVE COMMITMENTS THAT YOU HAVE MADE (blue cards)
#1	#1	#1
#2	#2	#2
#3	#3	#3
#4	#4	#4
#5	#5	#5

Worksheet 3

__ __ __ __ __ __ __ __

(yellow)

__ __ __ __ __ __ __ __

(brown)

__ __ __ __ __ __ __ __

(blue)

__ __ __ __ __ __ __ __ __

(yellow)

__ __ __ __ __ __ __ __

(brown)

__ __ __ __ __ __ __ __

(blue)

__ __ __ __ __ __ __ __

(yellow)

__ __ __ __ __ __ __ __

(brown)

__ __ __ __ __ __ __ __

(blue)

__ __ __ __ __ __ __ __

THE GIFT OF LISTENING

THE GIFT OF HONESTY

THE GIFT OF A POSITIVE ATTITUDE

THE GIFT OF ABILITY TO SMILE

THE GIFT OF COURAGE

THE GIFT OF CARING FOR OTHERS

THE GIFT OF COMMUNICATING

THE GIFT OF KNOWING YOUR
SELF-WORTH

THE GIFT OF BEING RESOURCEFUL

THE GIFT OF BEING ARTISTIC,
CREATIVE, IMAGINATIVE

THE GIFT OF BEING PURPOSEFUL
WITH YOUR TIME

THE GIFT OF PRAYER

THE GIFT OF HUMILITY

THE GIFT OF AFFIRMING OTHERS

THE GIFT OF DESIRE TO LEARN

THE GIFT OF ATHLETIC OR
PHYSICAL ABILITY OR FITNESS

THE GIFT OF DECISION MAKING

THE GIFT OF MORAL BEHAVIOR

THE GIFT OF ASSERTIVENESS

THE GIFT OF BEING A FRIEND

THE GIFT OF A PASSION FOR
JUSTICE

THE GIFT OF KEEPING COMMITMENTS,
ACTING RESPONSIBLY,
BEING DEPENDABLE

THE GIFT OF FAITH

THE GIFT OF _____

THE GIFT OF _____

THE GIFT OF _____

THE GIFT OF _____

Worksheet 4

V.   The nine life traits, which you placed on worksheet 3 are
     probably the most significant aspects of your life. God isn't
     asking you to throw your life away, but to transform who you
     are now as you discover a more fulfilling vocation.

     The gifts you have used in your life are all given by God for
     the vocation to which God calls you.

VI. Examination of the Biblical Witness
       "How can I know God's will for my life?"
       Sometimes we tend to want God's will to be too specific,
       too confining, too much like a blue print.
       The Bible offers criteria for God's will . . .
       OLD TESTAMENT
       . . . The Lord has told us what is good. What he requires of us is
       this: to do what is just, to show constant love, and to live in
       humble fellowship with our God (Micah 6:8, TEV).

       NEW TESTAMENT
       Each one, as a good manager of God's different gifts, must use
       for the good of others the special gift he has received from
       God. Whoever preaches must preach God's messages; who-
       ever serves must serve with the strength that God gives him, so
       that in all things praise may be given to God through Jesus
       Christ, to whom belong glory and power forever and ever.
       Amen (1 Peter 4:10-11, TEV).
     Discuss with others how these biblical criteria interact with
     your gifts and traits.

VII. The Ministry Potential of Your Life
     Discover the fullest sense of your vocation in these three
     stages:
     • THROUGH SHARING . . . focusing specifically on one
       person at a time, examine with your partner each per-
       son's life traits and gifts on worksheet 3. Share how you
       see each other's vocation from the data in front of you.
       You might want to take notes on what is said to you.

     • THROUGH IMAGINATION . . . place your notes from the
       sharing just completed and from Exercise IV in front of
       you. Let your imagination roam. Search for what is chal-
       lenging, new, and intriguing. Take your time and free
       your imagination!

     • THROUGH PRAYER . . . close your eyes and take some
       moments to direct your thoughts to God in prayer. Ask for
       insight. Offer what you have envisioned and imagined.
       Be open to small insights as well as any leadership that
       the Spirit might offer. Don't be afraid of silence or wait-
       ing.

Worksheet 5

VIII. As you consider your traits and gifts, what directions or callings emerge?

In what ways, new or old, do you feel God is calling you to serve?

In your current involvements, what can you identify as ministry?

Therefore, if any one is in Christ, he is a new creature; the old has passed away, behold the new has come. All this is from God, who through Christ reconciled us to himself and gave us the ministry of reconciliation; that is, in Christ God was reconciling the world to himself, not counting their trespasses against them, and entrusting to us the message of reconciliation. So we are ambassadors for Christ, God making his appeal through us (2 Corinthians 5:17-20, TEV).

Resource #3

Counseling Prior to Baptism/Confirmation

Depending upon your tradition, a personal response is needed when a young person makes the decision to be baptized or confirmed. This is the first opportunity that the young person has had to share a decision of faith in the public context of the faith community. It is an important moment and an important witness by the young person to other young persons, to younger children, and to adults.

In the congregations I have served, each young person selects a "faith partner," a baptized or confirmed member of the congregation, to assist him or her through the actual baptism or confirmation and to be a friend-in-faith in the years following.

Often I have one session with the young person alone when he or she has expressed an interest in being baptized. We talk together about the meaning of the decision, about the selection of a faith partner, and about the timing of the baptism (confirmation).

Then I have one session with the group of young persons who have announced their decision to be baptized (confirmed) along with their faith partners.

Nearly all the sharing in this session is done between the partners. I have used a variety of resources in both my individual sessions with the young persons and in the total group sessions. We begin by exploring the nature of a decision of faith in Jesus Christ. At the conclusion of the session we rehearse the actual baptism (confirmation) and answer any practical questions that the young persons might have about that.

I ask the faith partners to be with the young persons on the Sunday they are to be baptized or confirmed and invite them to whatever celebration is planned for the young persons following that occasion. In other words, the partners are integral to every part of the experience.

In the following pages there are four resources: "Accountable Love"; "Reflection Cards"; "My Statement of Faith"; and "My Decision." I have used these in individual sessions with youth and in group sessions with the youth and their faith partners. Each are handouts to be distributed to the youth. I allow time for reflection and personal response before we share responses together. The resources are flexible and can be used in a variety of contexts and in combination with one another.

"Accountable Love" Handout

GOD'S LOVE IS UNDESERVED.
I've done nothing to deserve it.
I need only receive the love from my Creator.

GOD'S LOVE IS ACCOUNTABLE.
God expects that I will view my life as a gift, not a possession, and that in all ways I will seek God's will for my life.
God holds me accountable, in love, to become a part of the people of God, the church.

In accountable love, these are the specific actions which many Christians undertake:

1. *Membership* ("I belong.")
   Joining a church and becoming baptized; being a part of God's people.

2. *Prayer* ("I communicate with God.")
   Seeking God's will through prayer; listening and meditating, as well as talking to God.

3. *Bible* ("I learn about the Bible.")
   Studying the Bible; learning about biblical truths for my life.

4. *Worship* ("I worship God in Christian community.")
   Attending regularly the public worship of God in my church.

5. *Fellowship* ("I enjoy being with other Christians.")
   Becoming involved with other Christians in a caring way; enjoying the company and support of other Christians.

6. *Giving* ("I can support God's work in the world.")
   Pledging of my financial support to the work of God's church.

7. *Leadership* ("I can be a leader among God's people.")
   Volunteering my talents and my time through the church.

8. *Service* ("I can serve the needs of others.")
   Offering to live out Jesus' command to "love your neighbor."

9. *Witness* ("I can share my faith with others.")
   Seeking opportunities to share and express my faith with others.

10. *Growth* ("God can make me a new person in Christ.")
    Opening myself, in all of my life, to the Holy Spirit.

I accept the ways in which God seeks to hold my life accountable in love and pledge myself to this by the grace of God.

_____
(name)

"Reflection Cards" Handout

I have used these reflection cards in a variety of contexts. On one side of a 4-by-6-inch index card is the Scripture, and the reverse side has two or three questions for further reflection.

" 'You did not choose me, but I chose you and appointed you that you should go and bear fruit and that your fruit should abide' " (John 15:5).

front

Are *you* chosen? Why?

_____

_____

In what ways is it possible for you to "go and bear fruit" with your life?

back

_____

_____

Jesus said, " 'I am the vine, you are the branches. He who abides in me, and I in him, he it is that bears much fruit . . . ' " (John 15:5).

front

As a branch," what is your relation to the "vine"?

_____

_____

What do "branches" receive from "the vine"?

back

_____

_____

"We love, because [God] first loved us" (1 John 4:19).

"No [one] has ever seen God; if we love one another, God abides in us and his love is perfected in us" (1 John 4:12).

front

What does this statement—
"We learn to love by first being loved"—mean to you?

_____

_____

What does it mean to "love first"? How is this a unique type of love?

_____

_____

back

If you cannot see God, how will you know God?

_____

_____

"My Statement of Faith" Handout

Respond to these questions as honestly as possible as a statement of your faith.

1. Why do I want to become a Christian?

2. How have I experienced God? Or how have I felt God's presence in my life?

3. Who is a person who has influenced my faith in an important way? How has this person influenced me?

4. Why is baptism and church membership important?

5. What have I learned from the Bible?

6. What is one of my most recent discoveries about Jesus Christ?

"My Decision" Handout

God has made the decision to love you.

You have done nothing to deserve or earn God's love.
You are loved just as you are.

What decision, in your baptism, are you now making?

There is no "one answer" or a "right answer."
Be honest. This is for "your eyes only."

Words of Jesus:

"You did not choose me, but I chose you and appointed you
that you should bear fruit and that your fruit should abide . . ."
(John 15:16).